Politicians and Other Animals

Olivia O'Leary was educated at St Leo's College, Carlow, and University College, Dublin, and trained as a journalist with the *Nationalist and Leinster Times* in Carlow. Her career as a current-affairs presenter began in 1972 with RTÉ. In the late seventies and early eighties, she moved back to print journalism and was parliamentary sketchwriter with *The Irish Times*. The eighties also saw her presenting RTÉ's 'Today Tonight' and 'Questions and Answers', and becoming the BBC's first woman presenter of 'Newsnight'. She also presented Yorkshire Television's documentary programme, 'First Tuesday'. In 1986 Olivia O'Leary returned to RTÉ as a regular interviewer and presenter on leading current-affairs programmes like 'Today Tonight' and its successor 'Prime Time'. She continued to further her newspaper links with the *Sunday Tribune* in 1994. She has won three Jacob's TV Awards and her BBC Radio 4 programme 'Between Ourselves' won a Sony Award. Olivia O'Leary was back on our screens in 'Later with O'Leary', a late-night talk show on RTÉ. During 2002 she continued to interview individuals who have made their mark on Irish society in 'In My Life', and her political musings regularly come to us from 'Five Seven Live' on RTÉ radio. She has also, with co-author Dr Helen Burke, written the authorised biography of former President Mary Robinson.

OLIVIA O'LEARY

POLITICIANS AND OTHER ANIMALS

THE O'BRIEN PRESS
DUBLIN

PUBLISHED IN ASSOCIATION WITH RTÉ

First published 2004 by The O'Brien Press Ltd,
20 Victoria Road, Dublin 6, Ireland.
Tel: +353 1 4923333; Fax: +353 1 4922777
E-mail: books@obrien.ie
Website: www.obrien.ie

ISBN: 0-86278-880-3

British Library Cataloguing-in-Publication Data
O'Leary, Olivia, 1949-
Politicians and other animals
1.Ireland - Politics and government - 1949-
I.Title
320.9'417'09045

1 2 3 4 5 6 7 8 9 10
04 05 06 07 08 09 10

Cover illustrations: Martyn Turner
Editing, typesetting, layout and design: The O'Brien Press Ltd
Printing: Cox & Wyman Ltd

For Paul and Emily

Acknowledgements

To the politicians, press officers, civil servants and academics who are decent enough to talk to me freely, I say thanks in the best way I possibly can: I won't mention their names. Many thanks, too, to the journalistic colleagues who shared their knowledge and experience with me. They are absolved from all blame for what appears under my name.

I am particularly grateful to the endlessly patient staff of the RTÉ library who have saved my bacon more than once; to Niall O'Flynn who as series producer of 'Five Seven Live' first persuaded me to do this column, and to his successor Conor Kavanagh, presenter Rachael English, and all the editorial and production staff of 'Five Seven Live' for their encouragement and help; to all at O'Brien Press, particularly Michael and Ivan O'Brien, my hard-working editor Susan Houlden, and designer Emma Byrne; to Martyn Turner for his inimitable drawings; to family and friends whose best lines and memories I have shamelessly stolen and recycled; and to Paul and Emily, who make it all worthwhile.

Contents

INTRODUCTION

Des O'Malley, the founder of the Progressive Democrats, isn't a man who hands out too many compliments. So I was flattered when, in my days as parliamentary sketchwriter for *The Irish Times*, Des told me that he always turned to my piece first.

'Do you really?' I asked.

'Oh yes,' he said dryly. 'I always read the ephemera first.'

That's what you get, I suppose, for writing about the people rather than just the policies. Yet it's the people who make politics worth watching. So that's what these pieces are, an exercise in people watching, a selection of random thoughts mostly about politics and politicians, recorded, on the day, for RTÉ's 'Five Seven Live' programme. They are written between two elections – from the booming promises of the 2002 general election, to the aftermath of the historic Northern Ireland Assembly elections of 2003 – and are updated somewhat for this book.

Many of these pieces are about the life politicians live, and if memories of Brian Lenihan surface all the time here, it's because Brian, more than anybody I knew, loved that life. In the Dáil, he would deliver his lines with all the manufactured fervour of a travelling player. He would then sit, mouth pursed in a silent whistle, eyes dancing, as the political brickbats sailed over and back across his head. He saw the Dáil as theatre (pantomime some might say) and, at its best, it still is theatre. One such occasion was the recall of the Dáil in 2003 for a special debate on the invasion of Iraq. The subject cut to the heart of so many current questions: Boston versus Berlin; international principle versus national self-interest; multilateralism versus unilateralism. Rarely have so many of the fault lines in Irish politics been revealed and discussed so passionately. Indeed, the situation in Iraq injected a new vigour into politics, both in parliament and on the streets, and I've gathered together some columns which I hope reflect that.

What's always fascinated me about politicians, however, and what I've tried to write about here, is why they do it. Why do people abandon a regular job, family life and privacy to subject themselves to the uncertainties of a political existence?

Reasons can range from Freud to family tradition, but the answer is best read on the faces of those who have won or lost on election night. In no other job do you court such public acceptance or rejection. Winning is like a drug. People become addicted to it, to being on the inside, to the possibility of power.

Watch TDs as they gather in the tiered amphitheatre of the Dáil for a vote. The ushers literally lock them away from the outside world and their chatter rises to a roar as they drape themselves over benches and kneel up on steps chatting, endlessly fascinated by one another and the life they lead, revelling in their magic circle. It's no wonder they seem to live on a different planet from the rest of us half the time. I've tried here to reflect that special world and its relationship with the public and the media. I've looked, too, at what it's like when politicians finally lose power, as Albert Reynolds did when he locked horns fatally with the one man more stubborn than he was in Irish political life – Dick Spring. After Reynolds's final broken performance in the Dáil, he left the Taoiseach's seat and stood looking up at us in the press gallery, a rueful grin on his face like an old-timer about to hang up his six-guns. 'You jump all the big fences,' he shrugged, 'and then it's the little ones that trip you up.'

Another selection of columns looks at the culture of different parties: Fianna Fáil's brash assertiveness; Fine Gael's fatal reserve; Labour's class confusion; Sinn Féin's surprising but welcome dullness. I've taken a look at party leaders: Bertie Ahern, Mr Consensus, a man whose words can mean whatever you want them to; Pat Rabbitte, a parliamentary star but yet to prove he's a polltopper; Enda Kenny, a nice man fighting what seems like a lost cause; and, the biggest political success of these last two years, Gerry Adams, whose party's electoral gains, North and South, leave opponents like frightened rabbits caught in the headlights. I've looked, too, at the men who want to make it, the likely lads in cabinet who enjoy themselves so much they don't even want to take holidays, even though we might all benefit if they did.

I've written about election times, which is when politicians hit their mad side. Dirty tricks are brewed up at midnight and pacts are made with the devil. Some people draw an ethical line in the sand and try to console themselves that they lost honourably. When they do, other politicians avoid them as though they're contagious. Losing is the nightmare they live with all the time.

These are politicians facing a changed society. Economically, the private sector has grown and state involvement has shrunk, and as a result those connected with the state and government – politicians and public servants – have lost influence and status in society's eyes. The power and good standing of the Roman

Catholic Church have collapsed and have, in the process, damaged the state and the governmental institutions with which the church was so inextricably linked. Developments in Northern Ireland have removed the North as a major political issue between parties in the Republic and have presented them at the same time with the new electoral threat of Sinn Féin. It's been a fascinating time and I've tried to reflect some of its seismic changes here – the new social and cultural confidence, the abandoning of old ways of thinking, believing and even speaking.

It would be a shame, however, if all this change meant that Irish people lost their legendary appetite for the sport of politics. There are few countries in the world that have the knowledge and the interest that we have in politics and political people. After all, it is the people, not the theories, that live. To paraphrase Goethe: theory is grey; life is green.

IT'S MY PARTY

The One Road

I had a great aunt, the youngest of four sisters, who lived in a staunchly Fine Gael household. She was a gentle person, and we feared for her when her strong-minded older sister died, leaving her alone in her late seventies. My father drove her to Mass the Sunday following the funeral and afterwards he offered to buy her the paper. 'I'll get it myself,' declared Aunt Nan, stepping down from the horse and trap. Minutes later she emerged from the local newsagent triumphant, waving the *Sunday Press*. After fifty years, Aunt Nan had finally come out – she was an ardent supporter of Fianna Fáil.

She made the best of the years left to her. She learned Irish, wore her Fáinne, wrote to us in Irish and passionately supported the party. And that assertive identity, that public declaration of allegiance, is very typically Fianna Fáil. Traditionally, Fine Gaelers preferred the Masonic signal and the quiet word. But Fianna Fáilers always took a public pride in the party badge. And they had their own world: their own newspaper, the *Irish Press*; their own language because, after all, they made it clear that they owned the Irish language; their own Trinity – God, Patrick Pearse and de Valera – indeed anything to do with de Valera was sacred. One friend told me her parents were especially overjoyed when her brother joined the Holy Ghost Fathers, because that was the order which educated Dev.

Fianna Fáil always regarded members of other parties as not properly Irish or at best tepidly Irish. Fianna Fáil's aim was to be more Irish than anybody and since that meant it had to be more Catholic and more suspicious of foreign influences, well, it was all that too. And Fianna Fáilers are still more Catholic (watch them make the sign of the cross at Dáil prayers), more nationalist, more populist, than any other major party, though if the Irish people change, well, they'll accommodate that as well. All in all, there is a ruthless pragmatism about them which may well stem from their military past.

They make a religion of being 'ordinary', of belonging to the people, the *gnáth-daoine*. They snigger at plummy accents, or social pretensions, and even the increasing numbers of lawyers, doctors, teachers and accountants who pepper their ranks are expected to slum it with everybody else. In Fianna Fáil, everyone serves their time. There are few examples, apart from Martin O'Donoghue, of new deputies being appointed to cabinet, or of deputies joining the cabinet before they have served as junior ministers.

They have also pulled off the extraordinary trick, despite having been in power twice as much as any other party, of portraying themselves as the underdogs, the outsiders. They feel they get a raw deal from the establishment media. They complain that RTÉ and *The Irish Times* are full of middle-class leftwingers who look down on Fianna Fáil. They complain that Independent Newspapers is full of middle-class right-wingers who look down on Fianna Fáil. And this from a party whose parliamentarians are now predominantly middle-class university graduates. With all the power they have, they still manage to present themselves as victims.

Fianna Fáil remains the most successful political party in modern Irish history and, despite the decline in its vote (as bad in the last two general elections as ever recorded, though nothing like the catastrophic collapse in Fine Gael's), a joint study by TCD's and UCD's Departments of Politics after the last general election showed three vital trends:

- Fianna Fáil retains better voter-loyalty down the generations than any other party.
- While both Fianna Fáil and Fine Gael retain the support of church-going, GAA-supporting country people, Fianna Fáil isn't suffering anything like the decline Fine Gael has suffered among young, urban, non-church-going, non-GAA-supporting voters.
- Fianna Fáil transfers less generously than do other parties but it, on the other hand, benefits from transfers and has recently started actively to canvass third and fourth transfers from known supporters of other parties.

Fianna Fáil also manages and spreads the vote better than anyone else. All these factors helps it to arrest decline, helped by the fact, of course, that so far it faces no credible threat from the opposition.

But what exactly does Fianna Fáil stand for? Well, it could be said that all great catch-all parties stand for relatively nothing – that's how they become great catch-all parties. But two things Fianna Fáil has always tried to embody:

The first is the promise of material success, and every Fianna Fáil leader including de Valera promised that. Despite his liking for maidens at rural crossroads, he started the process of industrialisation that Fianna Fáil is still pursuing. Fianna Fáil's slogan in the 1938 election was 'Speed the plough, speed the wheels', backing not just the development of tillage farming but industrialisation too. Dev may have wrapped his policies up to look like what the *Irish Press* in the thirties praised as 'Christianity turned into economics', but as historian and political commentator Professor Joe Lee puts it, you 'talk Christ and think money'.

Fianna Fáil knows that people may protest loudly about wanting better services, but in the end will that decide the way they vote? One senior Fianna Fáiler put it to me this way, talking about

the next general election: 'People will talk to their accountants –
and then they'll decide how to vote.' Which is fine, of course, for
those who have accountants.

The other quality Fianna Fáil stands for is an almost military-
style discipline, a hangover perhaps from the old soldiers who
founded the party. The party songs are soldiers' songs:

Legion of the Rearguard, answering Ireland's call,
Hark, their martial tramp is heard from Cork to Donegal,
Tone and Emmet guide you, though your task be hard,
De Valera leads you, soldiers of the Legion of the Rearguard.

And another favourite:

We're on the one road, swinging along, singing a soldier's song.

See them at Bodenstown, or Arbour Hill, or at the annual Feath-
erbed Mountain graveside commemoration for Noel Lemass, who
was killed in the Civil War. Fianna Fáilers stand to attention, chests
stuck out, like soldiers on parade. No other party does that, except
for Sinn Féin.

That's why the party is losing its way at the moment. Spending
cuts have replaced Fianna Fáil's traditional promises of material
success and, maybe more important internally, that legendary discipline has broken down. Under any other Taoiseach, mutineers
on the Hanly report would be out of the cabinet and backbenchers would be at once warned against rebellion, and heartened by
the possibility of promotion. If they judge that nothing will
change, they might as well kick over the traces locally on Hanly,
on incinerators, on stem-cell research, on anything that threatens
their seats.

'Bertie won't confront,' one Fianna Fáiler has been heard to say,
'and he won't defend. I mean, his use of the third-person plural in

relation to government decisions is just masterly. When people complain about a decision his government has made he says: "Did they do that to you, love? Is that what they did?"'

'It's about time,' said another deputy, 'that he behaved as though he's responsible for the country. The people who vote for us expect, at the very least, competent government.'

Fianna Fáil, more than any other party, believes in the cult of leader, but Bertie has made a career out of not leading. He lets his ministers decide and then take the blame. People who demand that he be forthright and decisive miss the point: for politicians like Bertie the trick is to put off decisions for as long as possible. That way you can avoid the consequences for as long as possible.

But what Bertie stands for is even more central to Fianna Fáil's culture. He called it his code of ethics and he explained it succinctly in the Dáil to the Opposition Leader: 'Deputy Kenny, you and I are around a long time. The code of ethics here is that people get in here, and try to stay in here.' Winning power and keeping it – now that's everything you need to know about Fianna Fáil.

Why Garret was Good

During one of the many elections of the early eighties, we were hurtling through North West Cork in Garret FitzGerald's campaign bus when we suddenly came to a stop at a country crossroads. A loyal Fine Gael crowd had gathered in the dark and the rain, and they crowded around the door of the bus to cheer Garret. A little boy was pushed forward with a present – it was a big teddy bear dressed in red and white. 'That's a nice teddy,' burbled Garret. 'And the colours, red and white, whose are they?' Party workers leaned forward to tell him but he burbled on. 'I know,' beamed Garret. 'They represent *Solidarnosc*, don't they? The Polish Solidarity movement colours, that's what they are!' In the silence which followed, the little boy looked at him in utter disbelief, and the bus pulled away suddenly to cover the embarrassment of a would-be Taoiseach who didn't recognise the Cork colours.

There are a hundred such stories about Garret, but it would be a big mistake to say that he was out of touch. Fair enough, he probably didn't know who won the Munster hurling final, or what had happened the previous night on 'The Riordans'. However, he did catch onto a new sense among many people that they wanted to look outwards, to the UK, to the EU, that they wanted to move on. Looking at Fine Gael's dismal report on its own future prospects, and at Garret's own book, *Reflections on the Irish State*, one was reminded of a time when Fine Gael stood for something. For instance, it was passionately pro-European, something which has been muted since John Bruton left, something which the government itself recognised when, in desperation, it welcomed Garret with open arms to the pro-Nice referendum campaign. In FitzGerald's day too, there was some attempt to address the intellectual issues and even the issues of conscience which politics presents. Mind you, on many occasions Garret wrestled with his conscience and his conscience didn't win. But at least there was a debate.

But most important of all for Fine Gael, FitzGerald was ambitious. John Bruton always behaved as though he couldn't believe his luck when he became Taoiseach by chance in 1994. And he seemed quite happy to go into opposition in 1997. And even though the party was a great deal bigger then than it is now, no party leader in a mainstream party should be happy in opposition.

FitzGerald never was. He pursued power determinedly. He worked at it all the time. He worked hard at his relationship with the press. If you were investigating a story he didn't like, he dropped a fresh story in your lap. He knew newspapers had to fill space and one scoop could replace another. And when you printed both stories – ah no, he didn't like that.

He was tough. I remember him on radio in the 1989 election when he brought himself and Joe Doyle in by a masterly bit of vote management in Dublin South East. Sweetly, they displaced the PD's Michael McDowell who, before he abandoned Fine Gael, had been Garret's constituency chairman. On the radio programme, Michael graciously congratulated him and pointed out that Garret had taken great risks with his own vote in order to secure the two seats. 'Thank you, Michael,' Garret replied bleakly. 'You see, some of us still believe in such a thing as loyalty to one's party.' Ouch.

Unfortunately, not enough Fine Gael supporters believe in such loyalty, or maybe they're just dying off. The party's big and medium-sized farmer base is declining and it's no longer clear what Fine Gael stands for. It may be, with what Charlie McCreevy has called a centre-right government in power, that social democracy is the defining way forward for the party. But if so, perhaps a merger with the Labour party would send out clearer signals than are sent out by Fine Gael in its present amorphous form.

Finally, of course, since the Good Friday Agreement, Northern Ireland is no longer the distinctive issue for Fine Gael that it once was. We now have Fianna Fáil criticising Sinn Féin, and pointing out stridently that Fianna Fáil is the guardian of constitutional nationalism. Indeed, it may be that Garret FitzGerald simply arrested temporarily Fine Gael's inevitable decline in a process where each new wave of constitutional nationalists pushes out the older ones: Sinn Féin replaced the Irish Parliamentary Party; Fianna Fáil is replacing Fine Gael. And in time, indeed, a properly constitutional Sinn Féin may replace Fianna Fáil.

The Trials of Enda

'Do you notice how Enda never laughs at Michael Ring's jokes?' remarked a colleague in the Dáil press gallery the other day. I had. Enda Kenny reacts to his fellow party member as to a mad relation who embarrasses him in public. When Ring starts his weekly circus of shouting at the government and waving his arms around, Enda looks fixedly in the other direction as though to say, 'He has nothing to do with me. I have no idea who he is, but he's definitely not with me!'

Now it's not like Enda to be ungenerous. He's an open, friendly sort of man, always supportive of his colleagues and even decent to opponents. But it must be hard for the party leader to poll second in Mayo to Michael Ring, noisy, cute and devilishly effective. However, difficult though it may be to swallow, Enda should be proud of the situation in his own constituency. At least Fine Gael has seats there, seats plural. There is only one other constituency in the country, John Bruton's Meath, where that is the case and a great desert of constituencies where there's no Fine Gael TD at all. Michael Ring is the least of Enda's problems.

Enda's a nice guy and that's important, to be the sort of politician people like. Some of Fine Gael's previous leaders haven't been like that. Enda may also benefit from the fact that maybe Fine Gael has got over its period of bloodletting. It's a real sign of a party in free fall when it becomes a serial leader-killer. It means members are reluctant to look at the real question of what they stand for. Look at the Tory party in Britain until recently. Disloyalty starts to make a party unelectable. If Fine Gael hadn't started bloodletting in 1990, Alan Dukes might be leader now. However, that's history, and Enda has to deal with the present.

He had a good war, so to speak, taking a clear and consistent line on the need for a second UN resolution against Iraq. His party ratings, however, have shown little real sign of recovery. But it was the news of the death of former Fine Gael Minister for Health and former Chief Justice Tom O'Higgins that reminded you how far Fine Gael had fallen from the glory days.

O'Higgins, nephew of Kevin O'Higgins, reminded one that this was the party which oversaw the setting up of the state; the party that declared the Republic; the party that held 69 seats in the 1980s, 22 of them in Dublin, many of them the last real intake of young blood: Alan Dukes, Ivan Yates, Nora Owen, Gemma Hussey, Alan Shatter, George Birmingham, the late David Moloney – all gone.

Now they have 3 seats in Dublin and only 31 overall. And (as it says in their own strategy review report – funny and sharp and well worth reading) they are associated with the gloom of the eighties period when they were in power, with memories of moving statues, unemployment, controversies about contraception, divorce and abortion, while the rest of society has moved on.

So how does Enda position them for a climb back against an almost permanent Fianna Fáil government? If he moves to the right where they are losing conservative voters to the PDs, will it then be impossible to do a coalition deal with their traditional partner, Labour? On the other hand, he could move to the left for the deal suggested by fellow Mayo man, Pat Rabbitte. Such a social democratic bloc would make sense, but would it not be dominated by Labour ideas with which Fine Gael would be instinctively uneasy? Aren't there Greens, Sinn Féiners and Independents on that ground already and, at the drop of a vote, couldn't Fianna Fáil reposition itself back there?

Once a party loses definition, it's hard to find it again. In a way, the Northern Troubles were a blessing in disguise for Fine Gaelers because the IRA always gave them a law-and-order raison d'être. Now their raison d'être is sitting right beside them in the Dáil, in a section of the seats which were once Fine Gael's.

I don't see any easy answers. What I do see is a decent man trying to do the right thing. And I wish him all I can wish him, something Fine Gael hasn't had much of, something no political leader can do without. I wish him the very best of luck.

Labour's Poisoned Chalice

'I'm not getting up,' he called from upstairs. 'I've just won an election and I'm not getting up today, not for you, not for anybody.'

His wife looked at me and shrugged. 'There you have it,' she said. 'If you want an interview, he'll only do it in bed.' So that's how Labour leader Brendan Corish spoke to the nation in February 1973, propped up happily on his pillows and surrounded by all the morning newspapers headlining Fine Gael and Labour's election victory.

Corish's sense of triumph was understandable. It had been sixteen years since Labour was last in office. But for any leader of the Labour Party, going into government is always a somewhat poisoned chalice. Labour presents itself as a party committed to equality and justice, as a party of conscience. Therefore a lot is expected of it, often more than the realities of coalition government can deliver. For Corish, the oil crisis and a world recession in the seventies meant massive growth in unemployment, and a real sense of betrayal among workers, and voters.

Economically, things weren't much better for Labour in the short government of the early eighties. And anyway, one has to ask how interested the then leader, Michael O'Leary, was in what was going on.

'I'm bored,' O'Leary said to me after an interview one evening, tossing back his quiff of dark hair.

'What do you mean?' I protested. 'You're Tánaiste and leader of the Labour Party!'

'Yeah, and I'm bored,' said Michael.

Few Labour leaders shared Michael's legendary attention deficit disorder, but did Labour ever have a good experience of government, one where the money flowed? Well, the money was starting to flow in 1992 but set against that was something else – Labour's decision to go into government with Fianna Fáil, about which many Labour supporters felt a bit queasy. That night, as Dick Spring arrived out to RTÉ for interview, journalists at the station began to tease his adviser, Fergus Finlay. Ruefully, Finlay described being embraced in the Leinster House corridors by a Fianna Fáil senator and ardent pro-lifer. Then, he described turning the corner and running straight into a passionate bear hug from Fianna Fáil phone-tapper, Seán Doherty. Life with Fianna Fáil didn't get any easier. The passports-for-sale scandal and the tax amnesty were only two of the issues hung around Labour's neck at the next election.

So where does a new leader decide to look for Labour votes? Well, the last election and the Nice referendums have some pointers. Sinn Féin and the Greens gained votes that might, in earlier times, have gone to Labour. Recent polls have shown an increase in Sinn Féin and Green support and it was in poorer areas and among young people that the 'No' vote to the Nice Treaty was highest.

Now, one isn't suggesting that Labour change its stance on Europe, but it has to find a way to connect with those disillusioned with mainstream parties. For instance, in the last election, there were ace political cards that Labour could have played, like the sleaze card. Labour hands on Dublin City Council were generally clean; Labour councillors had warned publicly of money being paid to councillors by developers.

Astonishingly, in an election fought in the light of the tribunals, these issues were hardly raised. Why? Was Labour more afraid of offending future government partners than it was determined to win votes? Should Labour therefore forget about government for a while and redevelop its own independent ideas and its own support base?

There are those who fear that a Labour Party traditionally committed to the role of the state has no place in today's post-Soviet world. But if Labour is above all a party of the people, it is perhaps worth asking what the people themselves are concerned about. One of the things they are concerned about is loss of community, loss of solidarity in communities. Much of this used to be centred on the local church. But the Church is disappearing now and the social network of voluntary groups it supported needs to be replaced by a more democratic one representing the sort of proper civic society which perhaps Ireland has never experienced.

Yes, I know, this notion of voluntarism or communitarianism has been picked up by right-wingers. But it can just as easily be a Labour idea, a revival of vigorous voluntary commitment to local communities allied with Labour's belief in excellent state services. It means asking people of all backgrounds to contribute to their society, not to act merely as individuals.

The French Revolution had a word for such people and no, it wasn't 'comrades' if you remember. It was 'citizens'.

Call Me Ms

I remember Pat Rabbitte on 'Questions and Answers' some years ago getting himself into trouble. The panel was reacting to then Education Minister Pat Cooney's refusal to use 'Ms' when addressing pay cheques to female teachers. Whether they liked it or not, they would now be addressed as either Miss or Mrs. The panel condemned this approach – all except Pat Rabbitte. 'Look,' he said impatiently, 'there are massive problems out there – poverty, unemployment, third-world hunger. Surely we have more to get hung up about than whether someone is called Ms!'

Well now, to say that almost every woman in the audience hissed at him would be an understatement. And the punishment went on all week. By the time Thursday came, he was chastened. Worst of all, he said sadly, was the little note his wife left for him at home, which read:

'Your dinner is in the dustbin.

Ms McDermott'

Now, Rabbitte refuses to be boring and he's complained that too much political correctness can kill lively political debate. So he ran himself into trouble again for the odd ill-judged joke that he made during the leadership campaign. However, the fact that he drinks in Doheny and Nesbitt's is not of itself proof of male chauvinism and a look at his record proves the exact opposite. Women star in his front-bench appointments, including the first Irishwomen ever in a major political party to hold the Finance portfolio and the Agriculture portfolio, Joan Burton and Mary Upton. And that's fair enough in a Dáil party which is, unusually, one third women.

But even as a union organiser for what is now SIPTU, Rabbitte actively recruited low-paid and part-time women workers, including contract cleaners, at a time when the trade union movement didn't take much interest in women workers. Even earlier, when president of the Students' Union of Ireland, he backed a women students' protest at Carysfort Teacher Training College, an institution which was run like a sort of nunnery. The students wanted to have the choice of different elective subjects than those being offered to them so they organised a sit-in which lasted two weeks. Pat and his colleagues brought in a heavy metal rock band to keep up their morale, and straight away the head nun called in the gardaí.

'But what are they doing wrong?' the gardaí asked the head nun.

'Well,' she spluttered, 'they're stealing. They're stealing electricity.'

Rabbitte has been accused of being aloof, and it is true that he has a somewhat episcopal manner and that his style of speaking has something of the bishop's ring about it. Phrases like 'sorry plight' and 'in the rubric' pepper his pronouncements from the pulpit. But the fact that he is at home with the formality of parliament doesn't mean he's not well able to get his sleeves rolled up and organise on the ground. For years, that was his job after being recruited by Micky Mullen of the Transport Union to expand membership into the public service, to white collar workers and others. He and his union colleagues would vie for the most exotic recruits.

'This week, I got the banana-ripeners,' boasted one colleague.

'That's nothing,' said Pat who'd been down recruiting at the dog track. 'I got the hare-starters.'

And that's the job in front of him, to track down and win the support of untapped sources – hare-starters, banana-ripeners and all. He has to take a more aggressive stance than in Labour's recent lacklustre years. Perhaps symbolically, taking his place as Labour leader in the Dáil for the first time, he took the opposite seat to that used by Ruairí Quinn, further away from the government benches and nearer to Fine Gael, better for a head-to-head confrontation with Bertie Ahern. He was sharp and succinct, taking the traditional Labour stance on tax and warning the Taoiseach that he should look out for attacks from his own backbenchers. The Taoiseach said he always wore his shin-guards. 'Ah, but you can't wear them on your back,' warned Rabbitte.

He knows he has to go on the attack and with the government facing into hard times, his choice of chartered accountant Joan Burton as Finance spokesman speaks volumes. Anyone who heard Joan and her husband Pat Carroll flay the Labour establishment at party conferences in the seventies will know that she can raise welts on the backs of her opponents. An authentic working-class voice, with an impeccable left-wing pedigree, whatever else Joan Burton will be, she won't be comfortable.

And what about Rabbitte? Is he left, or centrist? Well, Des O'Malley probably hit it on the head when he described Rabbitte as a moderniser. He doesn't carry ideological baggage, and he'll look for votes wherever he can – particularly among those forty percent who don't vote at all. Indeed, he may well notice that there are several people sitting on the independent benches who would fit very easily into the Labour Party.

However, one of the dangers in his becoming leader is that someone will advise him to be presidential and careful, like British

Liberal leader Charles Kennedy, who's become a solemn shadow of his former funny self. I hope it doesn't happen. Politics is pompous enough without Pat Rabbitte becoming too correct.

As long as he remembers, of course, that many of us to like to be called 'Ms'.

A Ballot Box in One Hand

Caoimhghín Ó Caoláin is proud of his lovely hands. When he stands up to speak in the Dáil, he produces them one at a time from his pockets like delicious bars of chocolate and proffers them palm up to his audience. Then, when he's making a very important point indeed, both hands are brought into action, one holding the delicate little finger of the other. It's an exquisite piece of hand-play, light and elegant, and totally at variance with the way he speaks.

To say that Caoimhghín is ponderous is putting it mildly. The words that TDs in Leinster house use are 'tendentious', 'pompous', and 'lumbering'. When he stands up to speak, the TDs immediately begin to rustle papers and talk loudly among themselves. The Taoiseach folds his arms despairingly and lowers his head, discovering a new interest in his big black shoes. Only Brian Cowen stares open-mouthed at Ó Caoláin, as though frankly incredulous that any living being could be quite so sanctimonious, and quite so dull.

And dull best describes the Sinn Féin presence in Dáil Éireann; deliberately, crushingly dull. And dull is fine. Dull is great. Lord knows we've had enough drama, tragedy and pyrotechnics from that quarter to do us forever. Because of that, deputies do their best to put up with the sanctimonious stuff – like being lectured by Sinn Féin about the need to get rid of guns. Still, when Caoimhghín Ó Caoláin declared during a debate on the Iraq war, with a total lack of irony, the need to decommission weapons of mass destruction, the whole house collapsed in laughter and Brian Cowen shouted, 'It never happened in your party.'

So far, said one deputy, the Sinn Féin TDs are suspicious of parliament and they behave probably the way Fianna Fáil did when they first came into the Dáil in the late twenties. 'They go around in pairs, a bit like Poor Clare nuns or Soviet sailors, on the basis that you must always have somebody with you to avoid contamination or seduction.'

In turn, deputies are suspicious of them – Fine Gael in particular. Fergus O'Dowd, Fine Gael TD for Louth, has called his constituency colleague Arthur Morgan a 'fascist' in a local radio discussion; and Gay Mitchell in a recent 'Questions and Answers' discussion goaded Gerry Adams about the killing of Mrs Jean McConville. Fianna Fáil and the PDs, with an eye to developments in Northern Ireland, take it more gently.

But all deputies, while they grant that Sinn Féin works hard in the constituencies, will grumble about the level of support these deputies seem to have at Dáil and constituency level; at the prepared scripts they're always furnished with; at the number of constituency offices they seem to have; at the money they spend on advertisements. Justice Minister Michael McDowell reflected a general suspicion when he asked if Sinn Féin's funding came from legitimate sources.

The other parties complain that Sinn Féin hasn't joined the club. There was great annoyance when Kerry Sinn Féin TD Martin Ferris mounted a protest at a GAA football match in Kilmacud against a game which involved Dáil deputies and the Police Service of Northern Ireland. Deputies were so incensed that they turned up from all quarters – some actually flew in – to take part and lend support for the game, and to pass the Ferris picket.

Sinn Féin deputies, in their turn, find the Dáil frustrating and its rules antiquated. It's like school, they say, with the thud of schoolbags against the wall as TDs head for their constituencies on a

Thursday. They find it interesting that TDs in other parties who will seem very adversarial in public or on the media will be quite ready to co-operate behind the scenes in the Dáil. And, predictably, they're astounded at the failure to think and plan on a 32-county basis even when the Good Friday Agreement has opened up such possibilities on obvious fronts like transport, tourism, and the utilities.

As they point out again and again, they *are* the only 32-county Dáil party and they lose no opportunity to introduce their Northern media stars like Gerry Adams, whom polls show to be the most popular party leader in the country. When they bring him in to the Dáil, which they do as often as they possibly can, they say people queue up to shake his hand, both staff and politicians. And it is he, not Caoimhghín Ó Caoláin, who is the face of Sinn Féin for all the young voters; his is the voice they heard refer so compassionately on radio to Mrs Jean McConville as 'that poor woman'. Younger voters don't remember the years of violence during which Mrs McConville was 'disappeared' by Republicans. And they won't be reminded of it by the new Post-Provo-type candidates being chosen for the local and European elections, like Trinity graduate and former Institute for European Affairs researcher Mary Lou McDonald.

And they won't be reminded of it in the Dáil where Sinn Féin keep it so predictable, so safe, and oh-so-carefully dull.

The Nice Party

There is a story about Charlie Haughey's last period in office, when pressures were mounting and he was beginning to wonder if it was worth it. At a table with a group of his colleagues, he asked their opinions, and one after another they said loyally that he should fight it out. Until, it is believed, he came up to his then most loyal lieutenant of all, Pádraig Flynn, who said: 'Ah, boss, you've suffered enough!' After that, Haughey knew what was coming down the line. 'I'm gone,' he was heard to mutter later.

Haughey's loyal lieutenants, the country-and-western boys like Flynn and Reynolds who followed him gamely, had been forced to go one bridge too far. And the reason? The PDs. For Fianna Fáil to break its rule of single-party government and go into coalition with the PDs was unforgiveable, and the country-and-western boys plotted to bring him down. So by accepting Haughey's embrace, the PDs had unwittingly helped to bring about what they'd always wanted – Haughey's political demise.

Funnily enough, they got on with Haughey. O'Malley said he found him professional to deal with. Indeed, it's said that when Harney was getting a hard time from Pádraig Flynn as his junior minister in environment, she complained to O'Malley, who wasn't very sympathetic but passed on her complaint to the Taoiseach. It was Haughey who sympathised, who put an arm around her shoulder, who said he'd do something about it.

Reynolds had no time for the PDs. 'Those guys are our opposition,' he said of them, and when he called Des O'Malley 'dishonest' during the Beef Tribunal, well, that was the end of that.

But, in the longer term, of course, the PDs have turned out to be Fianna Fáil's longest and most amenable coalition partners, so happy together now after six years that people are beginning to ask if they will simply rejoin Fianna Fáil. There's a very good reason why not. That's because, while most of the PDs' leading figures, apart from Michael McDowell, are former Fianna Fáilers, most of their voters are former Fine Gaelers.

There's a reason for that, too. Fine Gaelers who didn't like Fine Gael's swing to social democracy under Garret FitzGerald, and wanted to vote for a pro-business party, couldn't quite bring themselves to cross the Rubicon and vote Fianna Fáil, particularly under Haughey.

But the PDs are sort of purified Fianna Fáilers. A bit like organic vegetables, free of pesticides, the PDs are free of the rhetoric of Republicanism, and fundamental Catholicism, and all that populist association with the *gnáth-daoine*. These are Fianna Fáilers who are middle class and proud of it. Even a Fine Gaeler would be safe voting for them! Asked to describe the cultural difference between a Fianna Fáil Ard Fheis and a PD conference, one supporter said 'Well, Fianna Fáil's is like an all-Ireland final in Croke Park. Ours is like a Leinster match in Lansdowne.' The PDs are, after all, a niche party – they don't worry about trying to attract the masses.

When you talk to PD supporters, the words they use to describe themselves are words Fine Gael would have used decades ago. 'We are the coping class, the enterprising class; we believe in getting up and doing it for ourselves and being allowed to do it for ourselves.' They say they believe in the primacy of the individual, in individual rights and freedoms, in the private sector rather than the state, in low taxes.

They've always boxed above their weight. Their economic gospel of low taxes and less state has dominated government policy for years and now even the Labour Party doesn't talk about raising tax rates. Senior Fianna Fáil cabinet members like McCreevy, Brennan, and Cullen are ideologically at one with them.

They call themselves a radical party, but in fact they are a middle-class party. All their belief in reducing the state disappeared when free university fees were threatened and the middle class screamed. And it is that same middle class they have to look out for now. A succession of budgets have pushed more and more taxpayers, and more and more income, onto the higher rate of tax. While people benefited greatly from the reduction of tax rates, the clawback has now begun through the failure to adjust tax bands for inflation and through the many stealth taxes. Strains which didn't show between the PDs and Fianna Fáil in the good times will begin to show now, as the PDs step in to defend the mutinous middle classes.

Because the middle class is fickle and there's always someone out there trying to steal them away. Some PD supporters told me that as the crowd trickled in to a Leinster match at Lansdowne, a charming blonde man in an open-necked shirt handed out Fine Gael leaflets. Enda Kenny was trying to woo back some of those long-lost middle class Dublin votes. 'And were you tempted to vote for him?' I asked my PD friend. 'Nah,' he said. 'But I'll say this much for him. At least he knew where to find us.'

Having Words with Gerry Adams

The first time I interviewed Gerry Adams on television was in London for the BBC's 'Newsnight'. It was 1986 and the first thing he said live on air was: 'You know, Olivia, you and I wouldn't be able to have this conversation if we were both back in Dublin.'

It was a master-stroke. First, it established a bond between us. No matter how hostile I might feel towards him, we were both Irish. Second, it established too, before I could start throwing Republican killings at him, that he was a victim of censorship and that I as a journalist should feel uneasy about that.

Heading into 2004 he is Ireland's most successful politician. One clue to his political success lies in his adroit handling of the media. But that exchange twenty years ago gives a clue to the man, too, to his need to have his voice heard, not just because he's a politician, but because he is a writer. When you ask seasoned observers what Gerry Adams' ambitions are, they will say he has no personal ambitions, that he is a creature of the movement. Then they will point to his one vanity – his writing. He has now published eleven books. It's what he wishes he had more time to do. He's bright enough to wish he could do it better and he's rueful about his interrupted education, but not embarrassed. When one reporter pointed out to him after a press conference that 'distractionary' was not a proper word, he just shrugged and said: 'Ah well, words is words.'

The books are disingenuous. The only time we hear about Gerry with a gun is when he's shooting rabbits as a teenager. We hear a lot about what the unionists and Brits did. However, the La Mon bombing, which killed twelve Protestants in 1978 when, it is claimed, Adams was briefly Chief of Staff of the IRA, gets about one paragraph in his autobiography.

Adams denies he was a member of the army but Ed Moloney's fine book, *A Secret History of the IRA*, paints a picture of a master strategist both in the IRA and Sinn Féin. Adams comes across in the book as devious, manipulative, and cunning, and the perhaps unintentional result is that you end up being glad he was all of those things. Otherwise he couldn't have pushed his more militant colleagues down the road to a ceasefire. So now we have a ceasefire, but whether there are still illegal activities from which Sinn Féin is benefiting financially, well that's another question.

Adams has coolly usurped John Hume as the leading light of Northern nationalism and he's learned lessons from Hume. One is the need constantly to internationalise the problem in Northern Ireland, to keep it, and himself, on a world stage. Hume knew if he could push the problem on to a bigger stage, beyond the confines of Northern Ireland, nationalists would benefit. There's a cosy sentimentality about the way unionists often refer to Northern Ireland as 'our wee Ulster'. It's a phrase that evokes both fear and mockery from nationalists who are determined never to go back to that particular 'wee Ulster'. The burgeoning new nationalist middle class, whose emergence has been so brilliantly charted by journalist and author, Fionnuala O'Connor, want bigger horizons and many of them want the more aggressive political approach that Sinn Féin, not the SDLP, takes now.

Adams has been careful to tailor his message to include that middle class. Fionnuala O'Connor points out that Adams never claims, as Sinn Féin's Danny Morrison once did, that Sinn Féin represents mainly the lumpen proletariat of the nationalist ghettoes. He has never become too Marxist in his rhetoric and has always been a respectful practising Catholic, recognising that the Church is central to the identity of so many Irish nationalists.

Today's respectable Adams doesn't now include in his books the sort of republican skipping rhyme which appeared in his early collection of *Falls Memories*, and which went to the tune of the Perry Como song:

Catch a falling bomb and put it in your pocket,
Never let it fade away.
Catch a falling bomb and put it in your pocket,
Keep it for the IRA.
For a peeler may come and tip you on the shoulder
Some starry night
And just in case he's getting any bolder
You'll have a pocket full of gelignite.

Now, he runs a cultural festival in Belfast to replace the riots which used to happen around the anniversary of internment in August. He has worked hard to smooth down his rough edges and presents quite a dignified and cool presence in public and on television, as he showed when Ruairí Quinn unwisely took him on on the 'Late Late Show'. And as an astonishingly popular leader, he uses the publicity around him unerringly to push party hopefuls. 'In the picture, Gerry is always surrounded by the doughnut,' said one journalist. 'Sometimes the doughnut is Aenghus Ó Snodaigh and Seán Crowe running for the Dáil. Sometimes the doughnut is Mary Lou McDonald running for Europe. But Gerry's always in the middle.'

And the cameras will always follow him. So whether he's visiting a school or attending a women's political conference, he ensures that he has a new candidate at his side. More and more of those candidates are middle-class. The defection to Sinn Féin of former SDLP Coleraine Borough Councillor Billy Leonard, himself from a Protestant background, is an interesting indication of where ambitious politicians are seeing the main chance. Sinn Féiners have discovered they are very, very good at elections and in Ireland there's always one coming on one or other side of the border to ratchet up their vote and keep the party in the public eye and keep the ... um ... volunteers busy.

And has Adams got his own electoral ambitions, beyond his Westminster seat? Well, he's been putting himself almost above politics. There's no doubt that the party would like to have ministers in government on both sides of the border, and soon, but that's not the role for Adams. Nor is Europe, which would take him too far away. He sees himself as the vision-maker, the de Valera figure, dignity, glasses, books and all.

Talking of de Valera, you know, at some stage there may be presidential elections down here, and nobody spots the gap in the electoral, or publicity, market like Sinn Féin does. Now, has anybody spoken to Mr Adams?

POLITICAL ANIMALS

Why Do They Do It?

'Why do we go into politics?' mused John Kelly of Fine Gael years ago when I asked him. 'I often wonder if it's from an insatiable desire to have notice taken of ourselves, like toddlers who have been left too long on their potties.'

Why indeed? John Kelly was a brilliant academic who could have graced any university in the world. The Dáil has many such. Brian Lenihan, Michael D Higgins and Richard Bruton could probably also have had high-flying academic careers. Joan Burton could have made a fortune as an accountant, and Michael McDowell as a senior counsel. So why do a job which can be snatched away tomorrow due to the vagaries of an election; which is ruled by arcane procedure; which, for its impermanency, is only medium-well paid; which means you are on constant call to constituents; and which leaves you unfit to do anything much else afterwards? Apart from the politicians' stock reply that they want to implement their policies, the answer has to be, firstly, of course, power; then, the drama of living on the edge; and, finally, the addiction to that extraordinary love affair with the voter – the declaration by thousands and thousands of people that they chose you, you above all the others.

Watching TDs gather for a vote on the Order of Business in Dáil Éireann, I wondered at so many adult people submitting to a regime like that of some nineteenth-century boarding school. After the five-minute bell stopped ringing, they ran from every corner of the building, eyes glued to the monitors where the Ceann Comhairle had stood up. 'Oh my God, he's on his feet,' cried Fine Gael's Olivia Mitchell, abandoning her usual elegant sangfroid, and running like a hare for the staircase up to the chamber. Pushing in through the doors, they stood there, blinking like children who'd been rushed down half-awake from the dormitories upstairs. Then the doors were locked for the vote, and the members of the most exclusive club in the country turned to talk to one another. The noise of the chat built to a roar as backbenchers mingled with ministers, as Beverly Cooper-Flynn knelt up on her seat to chat to colleagues behind, as Independent Joe Higgins dropped down to talk to his friend, Michael D. Because the truth is that they are endlessly, endlessly fascinated with one another. They are all, in a way, competitors, but they also share something else.

'There is almost nothing harder,' said one deputy to me, 'than walking up to someone and asking them to vote for you. You can ask for a vote for other people without a thought, but when you ask for yourself, you're risking the most awful personal rejection. And so there's a shared respect among TDs, a sense of "Fair dues to you. You got elected too."'

'Just as, when you don't get elected,' said another, 'members avoid you. You're the ghost at the feast, a reminder of the failure which ends all political careers. You might be contagious.'

As in any school, the seniors impose the rules and obey them. Enda Kenny and Pat Rabbitte may find the bind of leader's questions frustrating. Seven minutes in all are allowed for each question to the Taoiseach: two minutes to ask the question; three minutes for him to reply; one minute for a follow-up; one minute for his reply. The opposition leaders dance the minuet, knowing they may be on the other side some day. The blow-ups in class come from notice-boxes like Michael Ring who is regularly sent out to stand under the clock; or from Independent Joe Higgins, an effective performer. The Greens are tolerated, but with suspicion, because they threaten the established parties. But Sinn Féin is an even greater threat and is feared and despised in equal measure. Sinn Féin deputies get the cold shoulder in the chamber or are hooted at if they criticise others for bombing and killing.

And yet it's so important that Sinn Féin is inside – well, half inside – the theatre of democracy. Which brings me back to the late John Kelly. One of the wittiest, most imaginative speakers who ever graced Dáil Éireann, he turned the pedestrian business of politics into the best sort of theatre. And Dáil Éireann, for all its faults – its rigidities, its slowness, and that increasing tendency of government to bypass it by using other fora – Dáil Éireann is still the only stage on which we see played out the electoral will of the people. It's the one place where the accents of Dingle and Dungloe and Drumcondra have equal status. There are other theatres, with louder, flashier shows – television, the press, the corporate world. But almost nowhere else can the players say: 'I went out and asked the people if they wanted me.

'And they said yes.'

Give Us a Phone

Bless me, listeners, for I have sinned. I once asked a politician to do me a favour. It was a long time ago, in an Ireland half of you don't even remember, an Ireland where you couldn't get a telephone. The waiting list was years long. There was a huge black market in phone installation. Houses were advertised, not trumpeting the claims of their back garden or their sea view, but the fact that they already had a phone. Except that mine didn't.

My politician, God bless him, said he'd see what he could do and a mere five months later, a blink of an eye in Irish telephone time, a Telecom man arrived at my house. He hummed and he hawed. He didn't know if it would be possible. Eventually he installed the phone and I thanked him with tears in my eyes – my hero.

''S all right, missus. Sure I couldn't leave you stuck, not in your condition,' he said pityingly, eyeing my eight-month pregnant body. Yup, pregnant and politically favoured, that's how you had to be to get a phone in Ireland twenty years ago.

And why? Because the state was incredibly powerful and only the state could dispense phones. When Albert Reynolds, as Minister for Posts and Telegraphs, stood up at a Fianna Fáil Ard Fheis and promised with messianic zeal that he would install hundreds of thousands of telephones, well, we cheered. Any man who could do this deserved to become Taoiseach. And he did. And with the phones, and with privatisation, and with an emphasis on the private sector as the real engine of economic growth, came a major move away from the old Ireland.

In the old Ireland, the state was a massive employer and a massive provider of services. It had huge control over our lives. New government ministers, with no experience of business or management, were industrial nabobs on their first day in office. I remember Mark Killalea, as a new junior minister for Posts and Telegraphs, looking possessively at every post van that passed him in the streets. 'Mark loves them little orange vans,' said a colleague. 'He thinks he owns 'em all.'

And in a way he did. They were like his personal Dinky car collection, just like other fellas had train sets and airplanes and telephones and even oil refineries to play with. And now most of their toys are gone – and their empires. In the early eighties, the state employed almost one in three of all those at work. It was an economic giant. Now, the public service employs just less than one in five of all those at work, and privatisation and competition has meant that the state's hold over services has almost disappeared. You can get a phone almost instantly with a choice of suppliers. You have a choice of airlines, of some bus services and of parcels services.

As the state has waned, so also has the power of those who control it, the politicians. We, the public, don't see them as quite as important any more, and we don't turn out at election time. Twenty years ago, voter turnout in general elections was 75%. In the last general election it was down to 62%.

Now, there are a number of reasons why politicians are less powerful: the EU and the European Central Bank make so many of our economic decisions for us; globalised multinational industries dominate the economy, dictating even socio-economic matters like trade union membership.

However, there can be no doubt that decline of the state as employer and service provider has also cut many of the old ties between people and politicians. I don't know whether the disciples of smaller government and less state – the McCreevys, the McDowells – foresaw that by their actions they would reduce their own influence. But the fact is we are not as dependent on them any more, and we don't take as much interest in electing them. They don't provide the quids, so we don't provide the quo. And that's OK, because they shouldn't be handing out favours. That's not their job. They should be shaping legislation.

So we'll probably never again turn out to vote in the numbers we used to. Is that bad news? Well, it could be that things are OK in our lives so we're not looking to politicians to fix them. Or maybe, in this new IT-led economy which grew up without the state, we just think we can get on the phone (now we have the phone) and do better ourselves. Maybe what we're saying to politicians nowadays is: 'Don't call us. When we're in trouble, well, we'll call you.'

A Special Relationship

Like Father McKenzie in 'Eleanor Rigby', the late Brian Lenihan had a selection of faces that he kept in a jar by the door. One was his mask of righteous indignation. This Brian would produce to great effect whenever he felt he was being cornered, and he used it once when I was pushing him in a television interview.

'My dear young woman,' expostulated Brian, 'I do not answer hypothetical questions.'

On the way out of the studio I tackled him. 'Brian, don't you ever again patronise me by calling me "your dear young woman".'

Brian reached for his other favourite face, that of injured innocence. 'Term of endearment, my dear girl,' he pleaded. 'Term of endearment.'

Brian came to mind this week when I was thinking about the relationship between journalists and politicians. Asked once what he thought about the UK press coverage of sex scandals involving politicians, Brian praised the Irish media. 'Oh, we don't cover that sort of thing here,' he said loftily. 'We're more like the French, you know. Men of the world. Men of the world.'

As Brian well knew, it was more Irish prudery than continental worldliness that stopped coverage of political sex lives. Even now, despite the growth of tabloids here, we're still not so keen to reveal the private lives of politicians. But what has happened over the last fifteen years or so is that the mutual respect that used to exist between politicians and journalists has diminished. As a politician put it to me, 'Politicians have become more wary and journalists more cynical.'

The relationship has changed, and that is mostly because the balance of need has changed. Politicians, as ever, need journalists, but do journalists need politicians? Journalists follow power, and power has moved away from parliamentary politics and even from national governments. The economy is now largely privatised and the state no longer wields the great economic power it once did. Control over so many social and economic matters now lies with the European Union institutions. Business and industry are largely governed by decisions taken by managements outside this country. Even national policy considerations are influenced more by the partnership process than by the Dáil.

Politicians have noticed that political journalists, who used to share their schedule and their lifestyle, are more detached. 'We have debates and business here until 9 or 10 most sitting days and there used to be a time when journalists would stay on long into the evening but now the journalists are gone home at 7pm,' complained one.

They complain that the pages of Dáil reportage in newspapers are gone, that journalists now have less sense of political history, of the context in which today's events happen. One politician described a conversation in the Dáil bar where the name came up of the former Fine Gael leader, James Dillon. 'And one political journalist there didn't know who James Dillon was!' said my politician. He wasn't shocked really – after all, how many of us really need to know who James Dillon was – he was just making the point that politicians, their predecessors, their whole place in history matters less to this generation of political correspondents.

But the journalist's life has changed, too. They're more middle-class, more of them are university graduates; they like to go home in the evenings and have a life, instead of hanging around the Dáil bar. Anyway, the Dáil is less interesting under Mr Consensus himself, Mr Bertie Ahern. Fierce commercial competition in the media means that no one can afford to give whole pages to the Dáil, and even prime-time coverage of politics is less than it was, say, twenty years ago. Also, as this country has grown over the last twenty years, it has grown away from public institutions like parliament and the public sector. Instead it has extended into the private sector, into business and industry and the whole increasingly commercialised world of entertainment and sport. The media is looking elsewhere for its heroes.

Its attitude to politicians is increasingly disrespectful. As Jeremy Paxman of 'Newsnight' says of politicians: 'Why are these lying bastards lying to me?' And that attitude is inevitable, looking at the evidence from the tribunals week after week, or from the last election, of politicians lying through their teeth.

As a result, indeed, the media should be indignant, but it should also differentiate between those politicians who cheat and those who don't. Disrespect, yes; indignation, yes; but not the prevailing blanket of cynicism. There is a relationship of healthy tension between press and politicians in a democracy. It's not a critical press which kills that relationship but a cynical one. Politicians, flawed as they may be, express the people's will. Their profession deserves better from those who cover it, and those who practise it.

Throaty Roars

With the Labour Party conference coming up, I got to thinking about party conferences in general and about the late Brian Lenihan in particular. Because Brian, you see, was the conference king, the warm-up man. It was Brian's job to work up the crowd for the entrance of the party leader and he'd get them so excited that that they'd cheer at anything. 'Sometimes the government has to make hard decisions,' he said at one Ard Fheis. The crowd clapped. 'Sometimes the government has to be negative,' he declared. They cheered. 'But we have to be negative,' pronounced Brian 'in order to be positive.' The crowd roared appreciatively at this pearl of wisdom and then party secretary Séamus Brennan disappeared, choking with laughter, under the table.

Party conferences are a bit like weddings. Everybody ritually applauds the set pieces, but it's the bits that happen in between that everyone remembers. Take Charlie Haughey's first conference where, an hour before it started, I came across a carpenter hammering furiously at the little stand attached to the Taoiseach's podium.

'What are you doing?' I asked him.

'We're raising it six inches,' he said. 'Otherwise, yer man won't be seen over the top.'

Jack Lynch's first conference after his 1977 victory is now remembered because his speech ran over and RTÉ television cut him off, a crime for which the station suffered for years.

John Bruton's first conference as leader is remembered because he shared some of his television time with comedienne Twink, whose gamey jokes are blushingly better recalled than Bruton's own speech.

Fianna Fáilers are best at the conference as rally. They're not too polite to cheer and stamp their feet and roar for the leader. I've seen fellas cry openly at Fianna Fáil Ard-Fheiseanna – a sort of daft ecstasy takes over because loyalty to the leader is paramount in Fianna Fáil, part of an almost militaristic solidarity, part of the great hunger for and will to power which is unmatched by any other party.

Fine Gaelers are much too polite. They never quite got the hang of the throaty roar. Even when Liam Cosgrave denounced in a notorious speech the blow-ins and mongrel foxes that the pack would run to ground, there wasn't a mass reaction. I met a Fine Gael councillor I knew coming out and asked if she wasn't gobsmacked by what he said. 'Oh,' she said, smiling. 'Gosh. I didn't really notice.'

But if you wanted drama, you had to go the Labour Conference. With Labour, there wasn't so much a will to power as a will to stay out of power. The anti-coalitionists were passionate. Coalition was almost always the issue and may be again. The leadership ran a gauntlet of socialist mutineers outside the conference, and socialist rebels within. Time and time again over the years the leadership was challenged, up to the point where in 1988 Dick Spring in his shirt sleeves marched to the microphone like an ordinary delegate to battle for, and retain, his control over the party.

This time, it's a bit different. Rabbitte is the first party leader elected by the party members themselves and an outstanding parliamentary performer. Labour may feel it's unfortunate that just as one of the Dáil's great speakers becomes party leader, RTÉ drops its offer of prime-time Saturday night coverage on RTÉ 1 from an hour to half an hour. That's not much more than twenty minutes, given time for an introduction, applause and the obligatory standing ovation at the end. Still, there will be the usual panic about an overrun, with press officers cutting the speech even as the leader looks desperately at the autocue wondering where great chunks of his favourite rhetoric have gone. One wonders whether Rabbitte, like Mary Harney, would be better to wing it. He's well able to, but that would be risky and today's choreographed, carefully staged conference takes no risks.

Imagine! A Labour Party Conference with no rebellions; no motions against coalition; no attacks on the leader; and a former mutineer like Joan Burton sitting on the platform as Finance spokesperson.

You'd almost wish that Joe Higgins and a few old militants could mount the traditional hostile guard of honour at the door, complete with pamphlets and megaphone. Ah go on, Joe. Please do. Just for old time's sake.

Going, Going ...

By now, they've all learned to do it, to pretend they're going gracefully. When the ousted leader of the British Conservatives, Ian Duncan Smith, emerged to make his little concession speech, it was well choreographed. His wife smiled brightly. His words were brave. By Monday morning he was on the BBC making a new start, pushing his new novel. But maybe the real Duncan Smith was the man seen heading for his car after the fatal vote, gesticulating angrily as he vented his hurt feelings.

It's traumatic, that loss of power. It's like coming off a drug. You've got so used to being able to control things – you don't even realise how much, until it's gone. I remember calling one day on former Taoiseach Jack Lynch, to request an interview. I left a letter with the Garda on duty but before I got back to my car, Mrs Maureen Lynch was out on the front path, beckoning me in. As ever, Mr and Mrs Lynch were hospitable, kind, friendly and no, there would be no interview. Over a cup of tea, the lunchtime news came on and suddenly, Jack Lynch waved his pipe for silence. Neil Blaney was on the radio giving his version of events leading up to the Arms Trial. As he listened, Lynch interjected sharply: 'Not true.' And a minute or two later: 'That's not true either.' And later on: 'Not true again.'

Maybe, I tried once more, Mr Lynch would like to give me an interview giving his side of the story. But no, he didn't. Right to the end he maintained a dignified and self-imposed silence. Still, that image remains with me: the man who was probably Ireland's best-loved, most popular Taoiseach sitting at home talking back to the radio – no longer in power, no longer in control of events, no longer in control of the story.

Sometimes that loss of power can change whole personalities. In his last day or two in power, Albert Reynolds lost all that cocky self-confidence which was his trademark. Albert uncocky well … didn't seem like Albert. As we watched from the press gallery, he stumbled through his final speeches, dropping pieces of paper. 'It was the shock of a lifetime,' he says now.

It took him about three or four months to start recovering but he wonders if in the long term he recovered more quickly than his family. 'Politicians are used to having to go out and face the world but your family isn't.'

Alan Dukes says the same. He thinks his wife was angrier than he was – and for much longer – after he resigned following a putsch in 1990. He went for long walks and thought a lot about it, and after about two months felt he was over the worst.

John Bruton thinks that the family may suffer more when a leader is being constantly criticised and under pressure, than when he is ousted from office. For him, after being voted out in 2001, the best and the worst thing was that the phone stopped ringing. 'Initially, it feels good, but the sort of people who go into politics are used to being asked things all the time so you feel a certain deprivation when it stops. But that wears off.'

It's a small club, that club of former leaders. Albert Reynolds remembers coming into the Dáil after the Fine Gael leadership coup to see John Bruton sitting all on his own in the restaurant with a cup of tea. 'He wanted to know how to deal with it,' said Albert, 'and I told him what I had done. And I suggested that like many former European prime ministers he should look at the whole European stage.' John Bruton appreciated it. 'I remember him coming over unbidden to talk to me,' said Bruton, 'and I knew why he was coming and he was very, very kind.'

Ruairí Quinn went immediately after Labour's poor showing in the last election. He meant to go when he was sixty anyway and he hadn't the energy to face another election. He misses taking decisions, but he says five days after he resigned he heard a story on 'Morning Ireland', swore, and went to leap out of bed. Then he remembered someone else would now deal with it. And that, he realised, was good.

But will they always be wounded, those who've been deposed, and will they hope in time for revenge? Well, they're polite in public; and maybe they really are forgiving. But maybe, being human, they're more in tune with ousted Conservative leader Ted Heath's reaction when he heard that his Great Enemy, Margaret Thatcher, had been finally thrown out. Ringing Conservative Central Office he said simply, 'Rejoice, rejoice, and again I say, rejoice.'

One of Us

When Charlie McCreevy emerges to brief the media after his budget, he is flanked on either side by senior officials from his department. Observe them carefully because they don't emerge that often in front of the TV cameras. Note, too, their demeanour. Compared with the bluff and cheerful minister they serve, they will be cool, distant, almost patrician. You want to know who the permanent government are? They are.

The brilliant series 'Yes, Minister' worked so well because a large dollop of it was true. Civil servants are a select and very powerful group; they do protect their own interests; they are intensely political (with a small 'p'); and they can run rings around gormless politicians. They are also, in the main, public-spirited, very hardworking, and patriotic. But let there be no doubt that they know their power, and it's staying power. One former minister told me this week about his blazing row with a civil servant. The official's parting shot was: 'Remember, I can wait. You are a minister. In time you will be gone.'

Former ministers say it was noticeable how the pace of implementation in their departments slowed down as an election approached. When the election was called, it was as though all the officials took one step backwards. When a minister's political aide commented on this, they grinned and said, 'Oh, you noticed that, did you?'

The speed and lack of ceremony with which they usher governments out of office was a revelation to one party adviser. Civil servants firmly presented him with cardboard boxes to clear the office and hurried him and his minister out the back door literally as the new ministers walked up the corridor. Nothing personal, just the business of power.

They are loyal to whoever is in government and they are not above relaying information about the last lot. In one case they pointed out that a former incumbent had one big weakness, that without lots and lots of sleep, he didn't function too well. Useful thing to know that, if you were timing a political attack.

Inexperienced ministers can be putty in the department's hands, one reason that Bertie Ahern was thought to be wise to give his new ministers in 1997 much the same brief they'd had in opposition – at least they had some starting knowledge. Taoisigh often found, too, that it was important to have party gatherings of ministers while in government. Otherwise ministers were colonised by their departments, going gladiator-like to cabinet on behalf of the department, and seeing one another as the enemy.

Civil servants get quite exercised about parliamentary questions to their departments and, according to politicians who have observed this, they will do everything they can to divert the question to another department. Ministers answering oral questions brief themselves on the first tranche of questions, not expecting that time will allow for more, and officials are said to take bets on how many questions will be reached. However, one minister remembers finding himself rushed into a whole new set of questions he hadn't prepared and was very grateful to have a civil servant beside him furiously underlining paragraphs and scribbling notes to get him through.

So who are this select group, the civil service? Well, there are about 37,000 of them and anyone who's had experience of them will say that in the main they work very long hours – and no, they don't, in most cases, get overtime. Sceptics would say that, since there is no measurement of output in the civil service, as there would be in business, only input can really be measured and these long hours are a civil servant's way of building up credits for promotion. The educational standard of most recruits is still Leaving Certificate, but more and more there are special recruitment drives for graduates at higher levels in the service. Promotion is still too often based on time served, and there are major questions about the success of the Strategic Management Initiative, the reform which was supposed to make the civil service more efficient and more accountable. One politician used to running a large department put it this way: 'They have learned to talk the talk of planning and business management, but often they have simply constructed targets to retrofit what they were already doing.'

Do they look after themselves? Well, yes. Public service expense rates for Brussels are highest because that's where most civil servants go. Mileage rates are higher for the first few thousand miles because most civil servants do short journeys. Pay rates used to be very low and are still low for clerical officer level but rates for senior levels have improved sharply.

Secretaries General of departments can earn over €200,000, Deputy Secretaries over €125,000 and you can look at the estimates every year to know how much we'll end up paying for them and their related pensions.

The culture of secrecy hasn't really disappeared. Faced with the Freedom of Information Act, many civil servants were heard to say that they would simply stop writing things down. One observer saw the phrase 'not a document' written across a paper, presumably to ensure it wouldn't be subject to a Freedom of Information request. Others were seen to stop writing notes in the margins of documents, and to write them instead on coloured post-it notes which could be removed when the file was opened to the public. When Fianna Fáil wanted to curtail the freedoms granted in the

Act, it handed the review job to a group of senior civil servants who, surprise, surprise, advised that whole swathes of documentation and correspondence be returned to secrecy, though the government itself went even further.

Civil servants now have to face Dáil Committees, which means they will be emerging more in public, and certainly their interface with the public in Revenue and in Social Welfare has improved markedly. But they are still wary of assuming a public face. While the public response to them is important, it's nothing as important as what the minister or other departments think. They know you must never, ever upstage your minister with the public, and that, just as important, you must not upset your colleagues in your own, or other, departments who will probably decide your future.

They have their black sheep, like former local authority official George Redmond. They have the questionable situation of senior officials with access to vital information leaving and going straight into the arms of the corporate sector. But then they also have shining lights like Ken Whitaker, Noel Dorr, former Secretaries General of Finance and Foreign Affairs respectively, and Dermot Nally, former Secretary General to the government, who have all contributed enormously to Irish public life.

They are an order onto themselves, and they are proud of that and of their generalist nature. They don't welcome outsiders – experts and scientists and professionals who have to be hired in every so often. One such person was informed that he was being given senior civil servant status to justify his large salary. But, he was told, he shouldn't lose the run of himself. 'You are not a civil servant and you never will be,' he was told firmly. 'You are not one of us.'

GIVE US A VOTE

Monkey Business

I was listening to Environment Minister Martin Cullen talking about election spending the other day, and it struck me that politicians and their supporters live in a different world from the rest of us, particularly at election times. They tear around, pushing election leaflets at us, but all the time looking over their shoulders at the opposition. Sometimes it feels like you're in the middle of the chimps' tea party at the zoo – noisy, wasteful, where they're much more interested in throwing custard pies at one another than in the effect they're having on the voter.

It's a sort of a mad game. I remember the big trick for one political party in our town was to grab the telegraph pole outside our house and put a large portrait of their leader on it. Then they'd fall around laughing as my mother, who supported the other lot, came out of the house and averted her eyes every time she passed the offending poster.

Nowadays it's a normal part of the campaign that one party spends time pulling down the others' posters. One candidate in Munster is suspected of sending teams out to deface his own posters and win him a sympathy vote. And there's a new wheeze since rules came in that you have to remove all your posters eight days after polling day. Now rival parties take down *your* posters, hide them and put them back up after the eight-day deadline, causing *you* maximum embarrassment and a fine. This is a really nasty one to pull on the Greens.

And that's the least of the chicanery. In one Dublin constituency in 1997, a high-spending candidate went around complimenting the people on their lovely street and their lovely houses. But if they voted for the rival candidate, he pointed out, she would change their area by bringing in thousands and thousands of refugees. Oh yes, she lost.

It's often not the rival party but your own party colleagues that you have to look out for most sharply. The big trick is to say that your party colleague is fine – that you're the one who needs the votes. Famously, in Dublin in the eighties, one candidate put out a leaflet claiming that, to spread the vote, the party wanted people just in that particular part of the constituency to vote Number 1 for him and then Number 2 for his party colleague. The only problem was that that leaflet went out all over the constituency, and the party colleague had to put out a rival set of leaflets to correct it.

Tony Gregory's first Dáil attempt was in Dublin Central in 1981, in the middle of the H-Block hunger-strike campaign. While Gregory had some sympathy with the H-Block cause, it was a contentious issue and it wasn't part of his election platform. Still, he woke up on polling day to find that overnight the constituency had been plastered with posters saying 'Vote No. 1 Gregory – support the hunger strikers.' The posters were stuck all over shop windows, shop doors – wherever they were going to cause most annoyance to shopkeepers, and they were most plentiful in the middle-class areas where the republican connection was likely to put voters off.

Gregory says he spent the morning fending off outraged shop-keepers and voters. He tried to pull down posters still wet with paste but, by that stage, people had already seen them and left for work – it was too late to undo the damage. He never found out who did it, but he missed the seat by 150 votes.

So this is what they get up to at election times. This is the sort of time-wasting, money-wasting, neighbourhood-defacing chicanery that election money often gets spent on, and now, NOW, Martin

Cullen wants to let them spend more money so they can do more of it! As it is, each candidate is allowed at election time to spend €20,000 in a three-seater, 25,000 in a four-seater, and 30,000 in a five-seater. These are big sums of money. One third should well cover the cost of your leaflets and posters – unless you go mad altogether, and some do. There are presidential-style campaigns run in Dublin, particularly on the northside, with massive full-length portraits of the candidate more redolent of Saddam Hussein's Iraq than a small western democracy.

Martin, however, has hinted he wants to raise the limits. 'It's not the limits that matter,' says Martin, 'but transparency about spending.'

So they can spend millions but as long as we know about it, that's all right then, is it? More money for posters that deface the place? More money for election handouts that end up in the dustbin, or the gutter? More money to give an electoral advantage to those parties who can raise it, over those parties and candidates who either can't or, on principle, won't? More money to create an unholy alliance between corrupt business and corruptible politicians, the sort of corruption the tribunals were set up to investigate?

Martin Cullen is a bright minister with some very good ideas. This, I'm afraid, ain't one of them.

The Face on the Poster

A couple of years ago, when Bertie Ahern and Celia Larkin were together, Ruairí Quinn defended the relationship. Ireland had moved on, he said. Indeed, who knew whether we mightn't one day have a gay or a lesbian Taoiseach?

It was an act of political chivalry which didn't do him any harm. The phone calls rolled in and one man in particular insisted on speaking to him direct. 'Are you Ruairí Quinn?' he demanded. Quinn said he was. 'Remember what you said about us having a gay or lesbian Taoiseach?' asked the man. 'Well, I'll tell you one thing. We'll never have a baldy Taoiseach!'

Quinn tells the story with a certain ruefulness. He's been long enough in the business of politics to know the importance of image – or to know, as Hillary Clinton once declared, that *hair really matters*.

In fact, during the last general election, looking at the range of aspiring baldy Taoisigh and hairy Taoisigh postered up across the country like a spreading measles rash, it was interesting to see how the hair issue was addressed. Bertie Ahern had plenty. Quinn's head was edged off the top of his poster emphasising beard rather than baldness. Michael Noonan's portrait cleverly edged him sideways into the shade – as a result a fetching shadow clothed the top of his head. The late and much-loved Charles Mitchell of RTÉ knew all about that trick. In the old black-and-white days of television, Charles would use a black marker to draw a line across the top of his naked pate to give an impression of hair while reading the news. Did we take him more seriously as a result? Well, he believed we did.

But back to the poster – there's always a subliminal message.

Bertie's portrait in shirtsleeves meant he was hardworking, a man of the people, a trick learned perhaps from the successful Eoin Harris election portrait of then Democratic Left leader Proinsias de Rossa in shirtsleeves, swinging his jacket over his shoulder.

Then there was the nice 1987 election poster of outgoing Taoiseach Garret FitzGerald working at his desk in the glow of a green library lamp. It was trying to tell us that this was a man who cared and worked for us, maybe even at night when we're fast asleep.

His family loved that poster – they have it hanging up at home – but of course it didn't work. Maybe there were people who thought we'd all be safer if Garret went to bed. Maybe there were unfortunate echoes of that great Stalinist lie about the lights being on all night in the Kremlin because Uncle Joe was up late worrying about the people.

Indeed, there was something a bit Stalinist about many of the candidates' shiny new colour portraits in the 2002 election. Mary Harney, who takes a good photograph anyway, had been airbrushed almost to the point of obliteration. Michael McDowell – well, maybe there's not a lot they can do with Michael McDowell. Eoin Ryan looked about five and a half and Gay Mitchell was accused of using his Holy Communion photograph.

'I had me picture taken only a few weeks ago!' protested Gay, driving around his constituency and fretting that too many of his posters had been blown away by the wind. Eric Byrne, who waited a few days before putting his up, was weathering better. 'But we are re-postering,' said Gay firmly.

Now if ever there was a man who didn't need to aid voter recognition in his own constituency, it's Gay Mitchell. He can't finish a sentence without people interrupting to say hello, or to beep their horns as they pass by.

Gay needed more posters? Rubbish! And that's exactly what election posters become – rubbish in your street and mine, along with the glossy leaflets through the door, the bags and hats handed out in supermarkets, all the electoral detritus which hits the bin.

Except that all this stuff costs money. When politicians were explaining in recent years why they took money from business people, they had a handy catch-all excuse – they needed it for electoral purposes – in other words for all the election gunge that litters our homes and our streets.

Imagine then an election world with no posters and leaflets, where politicians had to make direct contact with the voters and answer their questions; a simpler, cleaner world where contributions for electoral purposes could no longer be used a cover for corruption?

Imagine a world in which we might even be able to elect a baldy Taoiseach.

Looking after Number Ones

When Sinn Féin put up its huge billboard on the way into Tallaght with giant posters of Gerry Adams and Seán Crowe, someone had the gall to climb up and paint balaclavas all over it. 'And they would have had to get big ladders and everything to get up there!' complained candidate Seán Crowe. My heart bleeds for you, lads. Welcome to constitutional politics. It's a rough and nasty game.

Still, behind the election skirmishes, one could not but be conscious of the slow hand of history. Just before, in the elegant Round Room of the National Library, Dr Brian Feeney launched his book on Sinn Féin. It was from Sinn Féin, he pointed out, that Fine Gael and Fianna Fáil sprang originally and made their move into peaceful politics. No one from Fianna Fáil or Fine Gael turned up, and significantly, no one from Sinn Féin – they were all too busy looking for votes. And that's as it should be.

But still, when you're as old as I am, there's a sense of awe at how fast things change. Out on the canvass in Kilnamanagh, Seán Crowe's first message was: 'Use your vote. Even if you don't vote for us, use your vote' – this from what was once the great abstentionist party.

Now, mind you, the disaffected citizen who doesn't usually vote will more likely vote Sinn Féin, so maybe there's some party benefit in what he was doing. But in a way, Crowe himself is a measure of the new Sinn Féin. Neat, low-key, he spent time on the doorstep – ten minutes or a quarter of an hour – and he told his team to do the same. Twenty years working full-time as a political activist, he won over 3,000 first preferences in the 1997 election and a council seat for the area in 2000, polling better than sitting TDs. The housing estate we were in was one of the more comfortable in

Dublin South West and it was the second time he'd canvassed it since the campaign began. Five years ago, he wasn't pulling votes here. But the Good Friday Agreement changed that. Now, he was getting solid promises of number ones.

And what was the big issue? The North? The economy? No! One of the biggest issues was car insurance for young drivers – I kid thee not! And did Sinn Féin have a policy on that? Yes, it did, right at the top of Crowe's agenda. Sinn Féin would end the insurance company cartel and set up the state's own insurance company. At doorway after doorway, young men deprived of their God-given right-to-drive were reassured by Sinn Féin that they, too, would go to the ball.

And yes, the North did come up, among complaints about health and orthodontics. One man worried about punishment beatings. 'They're barbaric,' agreed Seán Crowe. The fact that these beatings might be carried out by Republicans was brushed aside as gently as the May blossom falling on Kilnamanagh's sub-urban gardens. Would the TV pictures of excavations looking for the bodies of those killed in the Troubles affect his campaign, he was asked. 'No,' he told the man on the doorstep. That happened during the local government campaign too and it didn't affect him. 'Who knows now who did these things?' he mused. 'Was it the IRA, was it somebody else?' More May blossom drifted downwards and was gently brushed away.

Crowe didn't talk much about the North. He was serious about this seat, which is why he had seasoned campaigners down from Northern Ireland to work for him, despite advice that it might be a mistake to over-emphasise the Northern connection.

But winning this seat, he said, would be even more significant than gaining Kerry North with Martin Ferris. The vote for

Caoimhghín Ó Caoláin in Cavan-Monaghan and Ferris in Kerry would still be seen as a nationalist vote. 'But with this seat we establish our credentials here as an urban, working-class socialist party – it would be a real landmark.'

The young men disappeared from the doorstep and his fellow canvassers were fretting – the Celtic *v.* Rangers match was about to begin. Crowe talked at length to some women voters and then gave in gracefully. He had the air of a man who had done enough. He had the air of a man who was going to win.

Up Close and Personal

And so the great election ballet lumbers to a close. All those carefully choreographed photo opportunities with the voting public are almost over, and to finish with, we have the full tutu and tights, the pas de deux, the great debate between Taoiseach and opposition leader.

Now the politicians and their handlers take these occasions more seriously than the public do. Before all these election debates or interviews, there's an extraordinary amount of scuffling in the wings in an effort to gain advantage, or in an attempt to put the broadcasters in their place. I remember Margaret Thatcher, before an election interview in 1987, objecting to the desk at which we were both to sit. The desk had to go and it was replaced by a low coffee table. Why? Partly, I was told, because she thought the desk gave me too much authority, but mostly because the Prime Minister knew she had very nice legs and didn't want them hidden.

Garret FitzGerald never worried about the interviewer, nor about his legs. Indeed, it's a sign of Garret's supreme confidence and toughness that he broke all the television rules and still survived. Despite all efforts to stop him, he had pieces of paper and pairs of glasses hung everywhere about him, the very picture of the daffy professor, until, of course, that hidden shaft of steel hit home.

Charlie Haughey was the leader who best understood the requirements of the medium. He didn't use television often enough because he was defensive towards all journalists and, of course, he had plenty to be defensive about. But he did understand that television is simple, and visual. He knew that you were always speaking not to your opponent, not to the interviewer, but to the voter at home. So he used simple phrases, language the average viewer would understand, and, interesting for a man with a short temper, he didn't let the interviewer rile him or divert him. He never brought a note into studio because he knew notes make you look down and people can only see the top of your head. He kept his head up, kept eye contact.

With interviewers, though, he played a cruel trick. He would arrive early, so you'd tear down to studio, pulling a comb through your hair, to find him sitting there immaculate, looking impatiently at his watch. Charlie knew all about putting people on the back foot.

Albert Reynolds, on the other hand, was fairly easy-going – his handlers would worry a little bit about the lighting, because if the angle was too high it could cast shadows and make Albert look too craggy. Albert's permanent tan seemed to obsess John Bruton who always insisted on wearing quite a dark face make-up.

In Bertie Ahern's confrontation with John Bruton in the 1997 election and with Michael Noonan in the 2002 election, the Fine Gael leaders were generally taken to have performed better. They were good at the adversarial set-piece, just as they were good in the Dáil. But this isn't Bertie's territory. Pat Rabbitte may have ambitions to be a parliamentary orator in the Trollope mode, but not Bertie. He's the great deal-maker, Mr Consensus, and he's uncomfortable with the cut and thrust of debate. Those big eyes, that sad rather than angry approach, make him a bit like a boxer who just wants to hug his opponent. He refuses to tangle. He defuses the drama of the big fight by seeming to agree with people all the time. And despite all that, or maybe because of it, he wins elections. Bertie may kill forever the tradition of the great debate once opponents work out that by hitting him hard, they did well – but by refusing to hit at all, Bertie done brilliant.

Fat Years and Funerals

I remember Justin Keating, then Minister for Industry and Commerce, sitting in the RTÉ make-up room in the weeks before the 1977 election and dismissing suggestions that he wasn't active enough in his constituency. 'I don't believe,' Justin sighed languidly, 'in going to the funerals of people I don't know.' Well, I didn't know a lot about politics, but I knew this much: here was a man who was about to lose his seat.

The funeral-men get elected. The people who turn up on the doorstep get elected. Yes, it's the nature of our multi-seat PR system. We don't have the luxury of the system in the UK where I remember Sir Keith Joseph saying once that he held three public meetings only in his constituency during election campaigns and that he felt that was as much as anyone should be expected to do. But take the constituency I live in, Dun Laoghaire–Rathdown. Only one candidate came to our door and that was Fiona O'Malley, and that was a good six weeks before the general election was called. I wouldn't have given her a prayer of being elected up to that point but I knew the personal contact would work.

Now, if you're a frontbench spokesperson for your party, you don't have time to do the footslogging that young hopefuls do. So the massacre of the Fine Gael frontbench has something to do with the fact that doing the party's business in the Dáil and on the media leaves you vulnerable to energetic newcomers. But still, at a time when the profession of politics is falling lower and lower in public esteem, you have to mourn the loss of people like Alan Dukes. It was his decision as opposition leader to support Haughey's minority government in its attempt to right the nation's finances. As a result he helped make it possible for them to lay the foundation for a decade of prosperity.

You have to mourn the loss of Alan Shatter, whose elegant legal mind helped to sharpen many a government bill. We'll miss Frances FitzGerald and Nora Owen, who pushed out the boats on so many issues but particularly women's rights. And the losses are not only in Fine Gael – we'll miss Mary O'Rourke who helped drag her party into the twenty-first century on the divorce issue – and Dick Spring, the Dáil's toughest cookie, who will always have a place in history for his work on the Northern Ireland peace process. You could build yourself a dream cabinet easily enough on election rejects.

But it was Fine Gael who really suffered, and not just because of funeral-goers and door-knockers. Call me dense but it all seems very simple to me. The government which presided over five fat years was rewarded by the electorate. The PDs were part of that government so they benefited. The idea that the electorate collectively gasped at the notion of a Fianna Fáil majority halfway through the campaign and swung like lemmings away from Fine Gael and towards the PDs strikes me as bizarre. It was always going to be the economy, stupid. The PDs were to bound to do well, and Fine Gael was bound to suffer.

Yes, Fine Gael got things wrong. It departed from its traditional stance of fiscal rectitude, which shocked and alienated loyal voters. The manner in which it got rid of John Bruton was bloodcurdling and a mistake. But its main problem has been timing. It wasn't in office when the coffers were full, and didn't use its time in opposition to face the fact of its own increasing irrelevancy. Firstly, Fine Gael was always the middle-class party. Well, Fianna Fáil offers an even better deal to the middle class now. Fine Gael support was always based heavily on the bigger farmers and the middle class who served that farming community – the solicitors, estate agents, feed suppliers, and all the range of grocers and hardware merchants and publicans who lived over the shop in country towns. But the farmers are disappearing, the big grocers and hardware merchants are replaced by great supermarket developments and the solicitors and estate agents and bank managers and accountants are now serving developers and business types more likely to support Fianna Fáil.

Secondly, Fine Gael has always traditionally peddled a good line in fiscal probity but even though it may come back into fashion, there is no market for puritanism in today's Ireland. Fianna Fáil has always understood that people are more likely to vote for you if you sell hope and the promise of material success.

Two things more: with the Good Friday Agreement, Northern Ireland is gone as an issue, and Bertie Ahern leads Fianna Fáil. Bertie is a funeral-goer and a door-knocker but more than anything else, Bertie is hungry for power. Who in Fine Gael, including those lost and lamented frontbenchers, is really hungry for power? Maybe a few more years in opposition will help them find out.

JUST BERTIE

Circular States

When the Taoiseach in the Dáil referred to Turkey as a 'circular democracy' we knew exactly what he meant. After all, *we* live in a circular democracy too. It's the sort that goes round and around and around until eventually the promises you made in the last election come back to haunt you.

Bertie's a dab hand with the foreign affairs, particularly anything with a Turkish connection. As a minister in Charles Haughey's government, he was called back from holiday in Kerry to welcome at Shannon that well-known Middle East statesman, 'Cyprus' Vance. Cyprus was obviously happy with his promotion from mere US Secretary of State to statehood itself because though Bertie kept saying it, he didn't correct him.

It's that special feel for language which was evident once more when Bertie said Mary McAleese had 'gardenered' a big vote in the presidential election – just a touch of Arcadia about it as though the President had gathered votes like fresh roses in a flower basket. Sweet, really.

And I suppose that it says something about us that we don't even blink any more when the Taoiseach murders the language. He wouldn't get away with it in Britain, but in the US it doesn't seem to bother them that their President is the sort of man who says he knows how difficult it is for ordinary working Americans 'to put food on their families'.

OK, so we're both Republics and less impressed by fine flourishes of rhetoric or oratory than the British are. And we pride ourselves on being less class-conscious than others, on not judging people by their accent or the way they speak – all laudable if indeed true. But it's still important that words, however humble, mean what they say, no more, no less. Words are the currency of politics and they must not become debased.

So let's look at this Taoiseach and his words under two headings: parliament and promises. Bertie doesn't much like the Dáil – he seems to spend as little time there as possible and it may be because he doesn't shine there, just as he doesn't shine in television debates, and why? Well, first because of the aforementioned difficulty with words; and, secondly, because the Dáil and television debates are adversarial in style and our Bertie doesn't like that.

He's a consensus man. He likes agreeing with people. One leading opposition politician has always complained that Ahern is the most difficult man to mark because he holds you too close, you can't get far enough away to land a punch.

But does that mean he really does agree with you? No, it doesn't. In the Dáil in late 2003, he agreed with Labour's Pat Rabbitte about the need for union recognition, implying as he always does that he had a special understanding of the importance of unions because of his background. But what do these words mean? He was never a union organiser. He happened to be Minister for Labour in the eighties and in that time and since, if anything, the problem of non-union houses has got worse. Only about 20% of the private sector workforce is unionised. If that didn't change in the good times, it's not likely to change now that we'll find it harder than ever to attract inward investment. So the words don't mean quite what they say.

But worst of all was the election. The government's economic sun shone right up to the moment the count was declared – that's how Bertie had ordered it – and then the rain moved in. All the things which had been promised in the manifesto: massive health improvements and medical card extension, better primary schools, 2,000 gardaí, infrastructural improvements – all these things promised and possible at the beginning of June, were disappearing by the end of June. Did those words mean anything? No, they didn't. Were we robbed? Yes we were. Will we remember at the next election? Well, *he* hopes we won't.

In the meantime, the consensus man is having to get used to saying no, and he doesn't like it. He's always tense behind the bonhomie, but he rarely loses his temper, which is why we remember his outburst all of eight years ago against Gay Mitchell: 'If you stop waffling we might get some work done. You are a waffler. You have been years around here waffling.'

As I said, he has a way with words, but when he's tense his mouth pulls in like a duck's ass and when he sticks his tongue in his cheek as he does so much of the time now, you know he's worried – worried that unless times improve dramatically or unless we suffer collective amnesia, well ... it ain't gonna be so easy for him any more, 'gardenering' them votes.

The Devil in the Details

I hope young Niamh McCarthy of Ballina got four photos of Westlife in June 2002, because the Taoiseach (who has certain connections with the band) promised her he'd see to it when he met her on the campaign trail. By the time his cavalcade had reached the east coast and Bray, he was still checking that Niamh had been looked after. Bertie always attends to the details.

Young people love him – he presses all the right buttons: the support for Manchester United; the carefully preserved North Dublin accent; the determined ordinariness. He must be the only European head of government who goes on package holidays to Lanzarote.

I remember when he became leader of Fianna Fáil I did a short piece on him for the front of the *Sunday Tribune*. On the same day his picture was splashed across every television screen and across the front of every newspaper in Ireland and some abroad. Later that week, as I passed him in the Dáil corridor, mobbed by journalists, he reached out and stopped me. 'Thanks,' he said. 'Thanks for what?' I asked him. 'Thanks for puttin' me on the front page on Sunday.' I was only a detail, but Bertie never forgets the details.

Now, you might well ask, how it is that his eye for detail would seem to have deserted him when he failed for years to ask where Charlie Haughey got his money from? Or when he signed blank cheques for Mr Haughey from the Fianna Fáil leader's account? And this from the same man whose sense of detail came sharply into play when timing an election to coincide neatly with the granting of a massive increase in child benefit.

But what's really striking is how this man of detail is conducting an election campaign devoid of any detailed contact with the voter. He may well have met every shopper in the country by the time he's finished his triumphant tour of supermarkets, but 'Hello, howaya' and a broad handshake does not constitute genuine political debate. When one cross woman in County Wicklow tried to raise the health issue, he simply smiled and his big black shoes moved on. In meeting him personally, you're really only getting the moving statue version of the Big Bertie poster. It's as though he's decided that his face should be message enough. Here's the face that brought you tax cuts, record employment, unprecedented growth. Gaze upon it and marvel, and think – maybe he could do it again!

It's not a relaxed face – it never is. Behind that smile, it's tense, driven, determined to control and determined that five of the fattest years in government will be allowed to speak for themselves.

But what would people say if they could speak to the Taoiseach? Well, I don't know because I wasn't allowed to canvass with him in his constituency, so I asked to go out with the brother in Glasnevin. Noel Ahern is shyer than Bertie, with a nice deadpan sense of humour. Being Bertie's brother may have helped get him elected in the beginning, he says, but it took him ten years in the Dáil before he reached the modest position of junior minister. 'Still,' he sighs, showing me his election leaflet, 'I get my picture taken with him every five years at election time. Why not? Everyone else does.'

And what did we meet on the doorstep? Angry taxi drivers' wives, distraught over deregulation (Noel blamed the PDs for that). And we met health issues over and over. But what spoke loudest was what wasn't said. The constant complaint of every election I have ever known had disappeared. No one said that they couldn't get a job; that their kids had had to emigrate; that there was nothing for them in this country. Significantly, no one spoke about the economy, no one.

All that may change drastically in two or three years time, but for the moment, as Noel Ahern ran from door to door, his trouser ends, like Bertie's, cascading over his big black shoes, he didn't question why this particular dog didn't bark. He didn't want the detail.

'I don't ask why, I don't ask. As long as they vote for me,' he said. 'I don't care why they do it.'

Second Term Blues

It was May 1997 and Fianna Fáil had been out of power for seventeen whole months. Bertie Ahern stood like a coiled spring in front of the television set, his arms crossed fiercely, his mouth pulled back into that duck's ass grimace which sometimes passes for a smile. He stared balefully at the screen where RTÉ's economics correspondent George Lee, in front of government buildings, was delivering yet more good economic news for the then government. 'Would you look at that, would you?' he protested, and you knew it wasn't George he was protesting about but the fact that this should have been Bertie's good news. Delivered on behalf of Bertie's government. From in front of Bertie's government buildings.

After all, Fianna Fáil always regards itself as the natural party of power – anything else is an aberration. It sulks in opposition. Indeed it's often a bad and irresponsible opposition, as Fine Gael keep pointing out as though being a good opposition was the height of Fine Gael's ambitions. No, Fianna Fáilers assume they have a right to government. They've been there for almost all of the last sixteen years and economically most of those have been good years.

Now it's not as easy, and that's not just the fault of the economy. Managing a second, or even a third, term in office is always difficult. Remember what happened the Conservatives in Britain and look at Tony Blair's government even now. Politicians become querulous, and tired. They can no longer blame the last government – they *were* the last government. Old rivalries fester and they start to turn on one another. Those who haven't been promoted, and, more important, those who've been demoted start to make trouble.

And it's happening here. There's fragmentation all over the place. Michael Woods blaming Noel Dempsey for stopping funding for primary schools. Micheál Martin and Charlie McCreevy carrying on open warfare over health. Michael Smith and others rebelling over the Hanly report. Séamus Brennan and Martin Cullen querying the ESRI report. Backbenchers kicking up over everything. And now the PDs, ah, yes, the PDs – because the PDs know rule number one of modern politics: beware the mutinous middle classes!

That's who they represent. No, don't get hung up on all that stuff about how they want to roll back the state. When it comes to state provision for the middle classes, the PDs defend it to the hilt. If they were a truly radical party, they would believe in state intervention only to help those who really need it. But instead, we had Michael McDowell and Mary Harney dumping early on the Education Minister to reassure their middle-class voters that there would be no end to free fees. We now have Michael McDowell, with an eye to his middle-class supporters, flagging his opposition to an incinerator in Dublin South East despite voting in cabinet to allow county managers, not politicians, to decide these things.

And there's no getting away from the middle class, not for the government, not for any party, because increasingly this is a middle-class country. It's not just that the middle class shout louder and vote more actively. There are simply more and more of us. And it wasn't just with Pat Rabbitte's conference speech that the Labour Party recognised this. It was Labour, after all, which introduced free third-level fees and they're now stuck with a spending commitment which will haunt all governments.

I think Noel Dempsey was right to want to redirect education spending away from privilege and towards disadvantage. But the middle class has almost all parties petrified. I mean, when did you last hear any major party talking seriously about putting up income tax rates? So where will the money come from to balance the books? Off services, of course, where else can it come from? From stealth taxes, and it's almost inevitable that we'll continue to see cuts in education, health and caring services. And though we'll all suffer, those who are least well off will suffer most.

In the meantime the government will worry about perception. As Bertie's brother Noel put it on RTÉ's 'Saturday View': 'We've taken the tough decisions. Maybe we haven't spent enough time at spinning it properly.' They can spin it all they like but whichever way they look at the economic news, times are going to be tough and the Taoiseach has little room to manoeuvre. He gave to the middle class in good times. Will they remember that in bad times? Ah no, the middle class never gives anything back and the PDs will make sure that they don't. It's enough to make a man want to take a sabbatical, except that our Bert doesn't like holidays, particularly in opposition.

So he has to wait and hope for things to improve, a man beset and besieged in government by what veteran trade unionist, the late Matty Merrigan, used to call 'the burgeoning ambitions of the bourgeoisie'.

THE LIKELY LADS

Brennan on the Move

Recently I was trying to get from Connolly Station to catch a train to Cork. There was a bus outside with no destination posted and I asked the driver whether it went to Kingsbridge. 'No,' he said. I turned away, and then a thought struck me. 'But does it go to Heuston?' I asked him. 'Yeah,' he said. As I went to pay my fare he asked belligerently, 'Do you have a pass?' I didn't, but as I sat down, it dawned on me what he meant. Only someone on an old-age pensioners' free travel pass would be so ancient as to call Heuston 'Kingsbridge'. Ah, Dublin bus drivers. Where would we be without their boundless charm?

On a private bus, maybe, where they're helpful and courteous to you. So when Séamus Brennan talks about introducing competition to Dublin Bus, well, no, my heart doesn't bleed. You can't move without hearing the word competition from Brennan these days and looking at all the familiar faces on the PD platform, my eye keeps searching for him. How many decades have to pass before I can get it into my head that Séamus Brennan is not a member of the PDs? He probably should have been one. He sounds more like one now than when the party was founded seventeen years ago. Because Brennan is an ideological refugee.

When the PDs were formed, initially an explosion of the pro-Lynch Fianna Fáilers who could no longer stomach Charles Haughey, it was assumed that Brennan, an ideological free marketeer and friend of Des O'Malley, would be among them. When he decided to stay on in Fianna Fáil, the word 'traitor' was applied to him in a way it never was to another O'Malley ally. David Andrews saw Fianna Fáil as a sort of religion. Brennan, it was said, saw Fianna Fáil as the best career choice.

In the years since, in a funny way, he's been lost to view. Despised by Charles Haughey, he served an undistinguished time in a series of junior ministries and then some senior ones. But since his appointment to cabinet, he's been a man reborn. He's been preaching a Progressive Democrat-style gospel of competition, competition and competition.

He despises monopolies. He's going to open up air and bus travel to further competition. Let the travelling public choose. It's not an idea which he was much associated with when he was Minister for Transport last time, more than a decade ago. But that was before Ryanair had forever settled the case for competition. Indeed, Brennan has been accused of trying to facilitate Ryanair by his controversial proposal to break up Aer Rianta into three independent airport authorities at Dublin, Shannon and Cork. But it isn't quite clear what the point of that break-up is, apart from allowing Brennan to flex his ministerial muscles. Neither has the travelling public seen any advantage as a result of his many pronouncements about the Luas. The mess at the Red Cow roundabout still remains a mess.

He will win public support, however, if he can prove through increased bus competition that he'll make life easier for the million commuters he's responsible for getting to work. That's why he's ready to take on all the unions, and even take risks with the partnership process, in order to get his way. And in the cabinet it's not only the PDs who agree with his free market approach: Charlie McCreevy, Martin Cullen and Joe Walshe would be of a similar view. By staying within the party, Brennan has strengthened its free-market wing, making it possible ideologically for the PDs, perhaps, to rejoin one day.

He's a born organiser – after all he had nine years as party general secretary and it shows in the constituency. In notoriously fickle Dublin South, he's held his seat since 1981 because he pays attention to detail. Before anyone had computers, he had a computerised constituency database. He brings out a constituency map with landmarks – all the schools, buildings and other goodies Séamus has brought or will bring to his voters. He has a formidable team who speak on his behalf at meetings: Séamus thinks, Séamus does, Séamus wants you to know. And he looks out for the last vote. On election day in June, a small figure hovered under an umbrella outside Knocklyon's polling station. The rules don't allow candidates or canvassers too near the polling stations anymore but Séamus, say observers, was just on his way out of the place – he was on his way out for hours and hours and hours.

As a minister, he has swaggered a little too often and fomented too many unnecessary rows to be seen as a safe pair of hands. But with his knowledge and experience of the party, he can never easily be written off. Watching himself and Martin Cullen walk out of the chamber the other day, neat, bright, committed, there was a memory of others like them – Charles Haughey, Harold Wilson, Napoleon. One shouldn't ever, ever, underestimate the ambition of small men.

Poor Micheál

In Cork, they have long memories. When Charlie Haughey made his first election visit there as Taoiseach, it was like Brutus returning to the scene of the crime. Here was the man who had murdered their Caesar and they would never, ever, forgive him. His reception wasn't just cool. It was hostile.

When we sat down to dinner that evening, it seemed like the waitress spoke for the whole city. 'I suppose you're down with Charlie,' she commiserated with me as though on a fate worse than death. When she returned with our wine she said, 'The cheek of him.' When she came back with our main course, she said, 'The cheek of him coming down here looking for votes!' People at the adjoining tables looked over approvingly. 'Looking for votes down here after what he did to Jack Lynch!' she said, delivering the vegetables with an indignant thump. Beside me, Haughey's man, the then lean and hungry PJ Mara, sank further and further back into the shadows. Sometimes it's wiser for the *voce* to sing dumb about the *duce*.

Well, Haughey went off Cork in a big way after that. The only senior minister from Cork City or county he ever appointed was Gene FitzGerald, for a short time in the early eighties. It was to be 1997 before Fianna Fáil recognised Cork City again, with the appointment of Micheál Martin, first as Minister for Education, and now as Minister for Health.

A lot of Cork hopes are riding on Micheál – Taoiseach, President, Pope, there's nothing they don't wish for him. Because they know, that, just like Jack Lynch, Micheál cares. Just look at that concerned frown always creasing his forehead; that worried air of a good child afraid to disappoint.

'Ah sure God help us, poor Micheál!' they sigh, knowing that Micheál carries all the worries of the world, and more important, all the ambitions of the people of Cork, on his slim and boyish shoulders. When Micheál wrings his hands over the problems of the health service, they sigh in sympathy. Poor Micheál.

It's just that the hand wringing doesn't cut much ice elsewhere any more. The expression of care and compassion was fine when you were seen to be ploughing resources into the health service – and he did. Health spending, increased by various governments since the early nineties, has gone up, as he ceaselessly points out, more than 188% since he came into cabinet in 1997. But when you haven't got the same resources anymore, the expressions of concern begin to sound hollow.

A new defensiveness has crept into his previously open interviews and, worst of all, Charlie McCreevy has him in his sights, riding shotgun on the Minister who just can't say no.

Martin hasn't been a bad minister for health. He's tried to be open, accessible, farsighted. But he made a mistake when he promised too much. To publish a vastly ambitious health strategy with no guarantee of long-term funding meant he was setting himself up to be beaten every single time one of its targets wasn't met. He also made the mistake of trying to fight his financial war in public. In the great Battle of Ballymascanlon nearly three years ago, he was briefing up to the point of going in the door, only to be humiliated by Finance. Those who live by publicity die by publicity.

Health, as Brian Cowen has said, is like Angola – there's always another landmine waiting to blow up in your face. But it's also vast and its problems repeat themselves. Health Service journalist Fergal Bowers recently delved back ten years to see what the problems were then. They were the same as now: waiting lists, health-board reform and more consultants. Martin might well argue that he's made a start on many of these through the Hanly, Prospectus and Brennan reports and the National Treatment Purchase Fund. But he might have been better to concentrate on one of them, for instance health-board reform or the consultants' contract issue, achieving by now some strategic changes which might have delivered what McCreevy, the paymaster, wants – more value for money.

Because it's going to get nastier. He'll be caught in the squeeze between health-service lobby groups and the Minister for Finance, and he'll be personally pilloried for every failure of the service. And the backbenchers, the ones who elect leaders, won't sympathise. And Brian Cowen will be building up his brownie points in nice, safe Foreign Affairs. And … ah sure God help him! Poor Micheál.

All Democracy is Local Democracy

Martin Cullen, if you're listening, this one's for you. You're bright and tough and you're one of the three eagerest new beavers in the cabinet. Yourself, Seámus Brennan and Michael McDowell enjoy school so much teacher can't get you to go home. I mean, did any of you even take your summer holidays? It seemed like one or other of you was always on the radio jumping up and down in your short trousers, announcing some spiffing new wheeze.

And fair enough. Any politician worth her, or his, salt is delighted to get into cabinet, but for what? Well, hopefully to make a difference. And you can. Do you remember the smog in Dublin? Well, I do and I remember Charlie Haughey telling a public meeting that you couldn't ban smoky coal in Dublin. Why? Because the old people were used to it, he said, and it would be cruel to ask them to change. And what happened? Mary Harney came into Environment, took on the coal lobby, and as a result of her ban there are no more of those smoggy days when kids in my street with asthma remain prisoners in their own houses.

So back to you, Martin. What about you? Well, you could do something really big. So big that politicians have been promising to do it for years, but none of them have. Why? Because it's the big dragon – the reform of local government.

Now, before you groan and take out your new catapult and start firing conkers at me, answer me this: why do people feel alienated from the political process? Partly because politics doesn't touch them in their street, and in their home, and why? Because there is no local democracy. Congressman Tip O'Neill said all politics is local. Well, it seems to me all democracy is local as well and we don't have it.

Decisions are made about our streets and our homes by power-ful local government officials and we, or our local representatives, have little enough say. Local elections have been postponed again and again over the years and no one makes a fuss because we all know that local representatives matter very little anyway. The county manager has massive power, particularly over planning applications. Where councillors might dare to vote against her, or him, they can always be threatened with being levied personally for compensation cases brought, for instance, by disappointed developers.

Wasn't that in the end what happened over the building of civic offices for local government officials on the Viking site at Wood Quay? Didn't much the same thing happen more recently on Cork County Council when councillors were warned they might face a personal levy if they voted against allowing the ESB to build pylons around the harbour?

We have, as Professor Joe Lee has pointed out, one of the most centralised systems of government in Europe. That centralised establishment doesn't trust local representatives so it keeps 'em powerless, just as imperial Britain didn't trust the Irish natives to run their own national government. The abolition of rates in the seventies made things worse. Now, almost all funding comes from central government so that we, the locals who used to pay the piper, no longer call the tune.

The massive power placed in the hands of county managers has if anything been consolidated by the 2001 Local Government Act, and the amended Waste Management Act, and this brings us back to you, Martin. The task of reform is massive, but at least you have made a start by ending the dual mandate which allows national politicians to dominate local representation. Make TDs do their legislative work in the Dáil and let councillors be councillors, on the spot, and let them develop the expertise now needed on complex local issues like waste management and traffic management. And now you're mounting a review of local government funding, though it will be interesting to see if it really changes anything.

But you should have gone ahead with the plans for elected mayors. At least, we would have chosen them. At least, they would have been there for five years and they'd have had a visible face and they'd have had to listen to us.

And Martin, I know there are all sorts of short-term political considerations being whispered in your ear. And I know backbenchers worry that local single-issue candidates could steal mayoral elections and that the reintroduction of local funding through local taxation could create a local power base from which they will be now excluded. But what about us, Martin? What about us? We, the people are supposed to own the political process, not the politicians.

What'll they say on your epitaph, Martin? 'This man did what his backbenchers wanted him to', or, 'This man made a difference to ordinary people's lives'?

You choose, Martin. You choose.

FLAGS AND ANTHEMS

Fighting for Ireland

When I was about fourteen, the Latin Mass was phased out and we were asked at school what we thought of the new Mass in Irish. I said I thought it was poxy, that it was a rotten translation and I didn't like it. For this piece of impudence, I was hauled in front of the triumvirate of nuns who ran the school and told I was unpatriotic. 'And your grandfather fought for Ireland!' they clucked. I was suspended from all recreation for a week. Sister Magdalena, who was liberal, stuck up for me, but I wasn't properly grateful because, you see, Sister Magdalena was Scots and her grandfather hadn't fought for Ireland.

Now, my nuns in St Leo's in Carlow were brilliant and there are many of us who wouldn't have jobs today if it hadn't been for them. They reflected the times, however, and in those times you didn't get away with criticising not just one, but two sacred cows, or, as they would have seen it, two distinguishing characteristics of being Irish: the language and the Catholic Church.

I remembered my little mutiny as we marked the eightieth anniversary of the foundation of the state. I wondered how many of the things our grandfathers fought for (and no, I still don't believe they fought for the Mass in Irish), and how many of the things they fought for now define us. The historian Eric Hobsbawm has written about the way in which many of the tools used to bind together a fledging state or nation may not be central to that state's sense of itself as it matures. So the flags, the anthems, the language, the folk culture, the territory, even the religion, may all be open to change once the job of state-building is done. I suppose from our point of view, the concessions we felt able to make in the recent Good Friday Agreement are an example of that.

What makes you Irish can be a complex thing. Working in England, I noticed some of the things that set me apart. For instance, like most Irish people, I think titles are hilarious, like something out of a pantomime, so I never take them seriously. Once on the BBC, I had to refer to a British nobleman ranking between a duke and a count, a marquis – except that I pronounced it the French way. We had a voluminous post. 'Get it right,' said one angry letter. 'He's an aristocrat, for God's sake, not a tent.'

I remember also the effect of the British Museum on me. It's a wonderful collection but somehow faced with those formidable pillars and those great entrance steps, I faltered. I didn't think I'd react like this, but I did. These were the gates of an empire, I thought, guarding all the loot from other people's countries. I couldn't walk up those steps. Eventually, I found it possible to go in the modest back entrance and see the magnificent Reading Room and enjoy one of the greatest exhibitions in the world.

So is this all that defines us, an instinctive rejection of empire and monarchy? No, but empire does have its effect. The English, for instance, are a joy to work for. Why? Because they plan everything. If plan A fails, there's always not just B, but C and D. And that's the inheritance of empire. You have the power and wealth to shape things, so you set out to make it work. You leave nothing to chance. You are a pessimist.

We, on the contrary, are optimists probably because, until recently, we couldn't afford to be anything else. Hoping it will be all right on the night is much cheaper than expensive planning. As a result, we get more spontaneity which makes this a great country to live in, but we also get a lot of cack-handed amateurism.

What we do share with the British is the sense of coming to a crossroads. The identity crisis which besets them as the empire fades also besets us as we withdraw from the empire of Church. We're escaping from the oppression of church influence, but we're also losing the vast network of services and spaces, the community focus that the church provided. We now have to provide that ourselves, for the first time to start owning our own state, to become adults rather than the adolescents we've been trained to be over the years.

Because what our grandfathers fought for above all, I hope, was freedom. Now, in a funny way, eighty years after the state was founded, we may finally have a chance to shape it as we would wish it to be, to decide, almost for the first time, what it really means to be free.

Play it Again

When Mary Robinson was making a speech in Chicago as President, her plane was delayed. She arrived late into a crowded hall with the band playing and people cheering as she was introduced. Suddenly, as she mounted the steps to the platform, she froze and stood there, rooted to the spot. The platform dignitaries stared at her. The crowd muttered. 'What's wrong? Is she ill? Has she got stage fright?' Then, after about thirty embarrassing seconds, her aides straggled to their feet, too, and then the Irish ambassador. What nobody but the President had recognised was that the song the Dixieland band was jazzing up happily in the background was the Irish national anthem.

Americans adapt things to suit themselves. Even the language in which the song is sung doesn't faze them. I remember one US visitor on an RTÉ radio programme saying how much she liked 'Amhrán na bhFiann', particularly, she said, the part about shoving Bonnie. When the interviewer queried this, she said: 'Oh you know, the last bit.' And she sang the last line of the anthem with her approximation of the Irish words, which came out as 'Shoving Bonnie around the field.'

I was thinking about this during one of the rugby internationals because the only bits of rugby matches I understand are the songs. I always watch the French because they have the *mère* and *père* of national anthems. The Welsh provide the greatest musical treat, without a doubt, when they sing 'Land of My Fathers'. But when I heard 'Amhrán na bhFiann' sung at Lansdowne Road with the same passion that makes Cardiff Arms Park such a scary place, I didn't know whether, to coin a phrase, it scared the enemy, but it sure as hell awed me. And 'Ireland's Call', the all-Ireland song for an all-Ireland team, was sung loyally by most of the team and particularly the Northerners. It allows them fairly comfortably to say who they are, and that's what anthems are about.

Now, the tussle over the Irish national anthem goes back a long way. For the first four years of the state we didn't have an anthem, not officially. A number of songs, including 'God Save Ireland' and 'A Nation Once Again', were played. When a decision had to be made as to what would be played at the 1924 Olympic Games in Paris, Seán Lester, then Director of Publicity at the Department of External Affairs, advised the government to opt for Thomas Moore's gentle ballad 'Let Erin Remember'. It would be a better choice for playing abroad than the 'Soldier's Song' or 'A Nation Once Again' which, he thought, were 'hardly suitable' either in words or music. He advised the Cosgrave government to hold a competition for a new anthem or new words to 'Let Erin Remember'. But the more militant 'Soldier's Song' continued to be played at home. Since it was written in 1907 by Peadar Kearney (Brendan Behan's uncle) and Patrick Heaney, it had become the marching song of the Irish Volunteers. However, many felt then, as many do now, that the words were too bloody to include all traditions – words like 'mid cannon's roar and rifle's peal, we'll sing the soldier's song.'

Risteard Mulcahy, who was then Chief of Staff, is reported as claiming that he dates its acceptance from an evening when he turned up with colleagues in an official box at the Gaiety Theatre. They were in uniform, with their army caps bearing the intertwined FF insignia – *'Fianna'* from the ancient third-century military organisation, and *'Fáil'* meaning 'destiny'. The orchestra struck up 'Amhrán na bhFiann' with its opening line: 'Sinne Fianna Fáil'. The press then speculated that this was a sign that 'Amhrán na bhFiann' was to be the official anthem, and effectively that is what it became in 1926 except for where 'God Save the King' was played in certain circles to receive the Governor General.

Fine Gael, understandably, were always uncomfortable about those opening lines, so when they came into office in 1948 they changed the phrase 'Fianna Fáil' to 'Laochra Fáil'. And then Dev changed it back in 1951. Then Fine Gael changed it back in 1954, and after Dev changed it back in 1957, Fine Gael gave up. And now we sing it lustily and happily despite some of its associations and its bloody words.

In some countries, of course, the historic associations with national anthems have been truly horrific but the tunes themselves remain. The Germans sing their Hayden hymn without its Third-Reich associated first verse declaring, 'Deutschland, Deutschland über Alles'. After Stalin, the Soviets took out references to him but still kept their resonant national tune. Anthems offer a continuity, a statement of national identity despite the crimes of some national rulers.

And yes, the Iraqis have a national anthem. It's short and it starts very like the French Marseillaise. Iraqi children used to sing it when they raised the national flag at school. Despite some of its associations, it means home and homeland to them.

That is why looking at the indignant crowd who pushed past the British to bring relief supplies to their relations in Basra during the invasion of Iraq, or hearing them now demand their own government, you wonder why anyone should be surprised at their anger.

They don't want strangers telling them what to do in their own country. Their families, their cities, their sovereignty have been invaded. We stand up and sing proudly to say who we are. Why should anyone be surprised to find that they do too?

Location, Location

There's a story, perhaps apocryphal, about an eminent member of the Bar in Dublin who was a bit put out by an upmarket housing development on the small lane on which he lived. When the houses were almost built, the advertising hoardings went up renaming the place as Manor Park or something equally pretentious, and our barrister insisted that the local authority should have a poll of residents to decide the name of the lane. The poll was completed with the one resident voting – that was him – and the address became New Fatima Mansions.

Addresses are always a sensitive issue, and the case at the Mahon Tribunal of the builder who paid Liam Lawlor to save him from falling from Lucan into Clondalkin reflects a real property owners' and sellers' paranoia about their address and their postal designation. Take a big housing development off the Navan Road. Originally it had one entrance onto the Dublin 15, or Castleknock, side and, since it is the entrance which decides these things, the estate was designated as being in Dublin 15. For the convenience of residents, however, the developers broke in an entrance on the other side, so logically speaking, some of the houses should now be designated Dublin 11. It seems simple, really, except that all hell broke loose and residents, TDs and councillors besieged An Post. Why? Because Dublin 11 includes Finglas.

People go to a lot of lengths to hang on to what they think is a good address. The Marley Park area of Rathfarnham used to be Dublin 14 until about sixteen years ago when a new postal delivery office was built and the area became Dublin 16. Some people, however, still give their address as Dublin 14, clinging to what they see as the old, posher designation even though it means that their post is always a day late because it goes first to Dundrum.

Rathfarnham itself is a desirable area, indeed to some people it's not so much an area as a concept. The Advertising Standards Authority investigated a complaint in recent years that an estate was advertised as being 'in a perfect parkside setting in Rathfarnham'. When it was discovered that the estate was not properly speaking in Rathfarnham at all, the excuse was given that, 'Oh well, people *felt* they were in Rathfarnham.' So there!

Rathfarnham is the answer to our cyberspace age: a virtual address, a state of being. Does that mean that a three-bedroom house there is cheaper, or dearer, I wonder?

An address in County Dublin carries more kudos and a higher property price – after all, to go back to the Lucan–Clondalkin row, Lucan is in County Dublin and Clondalkin is not. Most of Foxrock used to be in the county but is now in Dublin 18. However, you still find people clinging to their County Dublin address, or asking, 'But do you live in proper Foxrock?' – meaning the mansions of Westminster Road rather than the comfortable housing estates of Foxrock Park (which really, my dear, is almost Dean's Grange).

Then there was the battle of Dublin 6. Sixteen years ago a new postal delivery office was built in the Terenure area and the new territory it covered was to be called Dublin 12. However, some people were wedded to Dublin 6 and the connection with Rathgar and Rathmines, so the compromise was this strange and unique designation of Dublin 6 west. Recently, there was a suggestion that Knocklyon, which is in Dublin 16, should go into Dublin 24 which includes Tallaght. But after the usual rush of protests from TDs and residents' associations, nothing changed.

Much of the tension about addresses in Dublin arises in the areas of new development to the west. There are many who would say that the big divide in Dublin is no longer north–south, but between the expanded, under-serviced west and the spoiled, settled east. As one woman from west Dublin put it: 'I wish I lived along the east coast and then I, too, could have the luxury of moaning about how awful it is not to have the DART at weekends!'

As for me, ah sure, what would I know? I don't even come from here. I'm a culchie.

Mincing Words

I know I *look* out of date. My daughter shudders often enough and says, 'Gawd, Mum – not the shoulder pads!' But I never thought I'd so quickly *sound* out of date. People with big round vowels – and mine are bigger and rounder since I come from the country – are almost an anachronism. All around me, the under thirty-fives are speaking a foreign language and I'm constantly asking, 'What did they say?'

I think it first really hit me during the Bosnian crisis in the early nineties when I heard someone on the radio mention the need for 'humanitarian car doors'. Now having been caught in many a cruel car door myself, I could see this was a good idea but hardly an answer to Bosnia's problems – until I realised that the young presenter was talking about 'humanitarian corridors'.

Only a few weeks ago, in a television programme about the development of hypermarkets in Ireland, a young whizz kid mentioned Ashtown shopping. I wondered where Ashtown was until it struck me she was talking about *out of town* shopping. Now, I'm not attacking younger people – I have one in the house, or should I say 'hass'. I'm just trying to understand them, and conscious that as I get older and deafer, I'll be totally confused by elided syllables and unpredictable vowels. But I'll have to learn, because this extraordinary accent which strangles every vowel sound known to humankind is spreading faster than the DART, after which it's called.

It's our version of Estuary English, that Cockney-influenced English of the South East which is spreading across Britain. In Estuary English, a middle or final 't' is lost to a glottal stop and the 'l' becomes a sort of 'w'. So, football becomes foo'bow and places we fly to become Ga'wick, Sco'and and of course Lu'on Ae'poh. It's already affected the standard English of Received Pronunciation. No longer do posh newsreaders speak as though a crèche was something that happened on the M1, nor do announcers in railway stations tell you as you board a train to 'mend the gep'. A recent survey of the Queen's broadcasts have noticed her vowels relaxing, moving from calling her only daughter 'Enn' to what the Princess herself says, Anne.

The old accent in Britain was a way of standardising upper-class-speak. Top people spoke the same way whether they were from London, or Leeds or Glasgow. You excluded yourself by speaking with a regional accent. Estuary English is more democratic because everyone sounds the same no matter what class they're from – which is fine, but means that regional accents may be in danger of disappearing.

I think that's a pity, there and here. We've already lost the luxurious old Dublin drawl. You remember the way Noel Purcell and his accompanist, the wonderful Peggy Dell, used to speak? The actor, David Kelly, and journalist, Cathal O'Shannon, still have that accent – slow and ironic, and sometimes faintly menacing.

But today, in DART-speak, everything is fast and elided and most vowels are flattened beyond recognition. As a result, the 'ow' sound becomes 'a': 'roundabout' becomes 'rahndabaht'; 'county council' becomes 'canty cancil'. The 'eh' sound becomes 'a', too, so 'investment' and 'recession' have become 'invastment' and 'racassion'. And the big round 'o' has gone completely – growth has become 'grith'.

All those examples come from young people in their twenties and thirties, but where did they pick it up? Estuary English in Britain is believed to have come from the generations of kids subjected to the cheery young Cockney presenters of children's programmes. But where did ours come from? Well, some is estuary pronunciation. Note how people in London also now talk of 'tan' instead of 'town', and 'bran' instead of 'brown'.

However, another very particular television influence was brought to bear here. All those north-of-Ireland accents in thirty years of RTÉ's massive coverage of the North must have affected the under thirty-fives. Up there they narrow their broad vowels: not 'how now brown cow' but 'hi ni brine ci', and they flatten their narrow vowels. They talk of 'Caltic' football club and of 'cradit cards'. Sound familiar?

Nationalists down here always thought we'd end up taking over the North. It may be that *they* are already colonising the way we speak. A perfect example of the flattened vowels we're getting used to comes in a story told by Michael Keane of the *Press* who was once ordering dinner in Belfast's Europa Hotel. 'I might have prawns,' he said. 'What are the prawns like?' The waitress gave him a pitying look and then she told him: 'They're wee pank fash.'

Loss and Lissadell

As you walk up the elegant staircase to the Seanad in Leinster House, you are confronted by the portrait of a lady. Set in among the beautiful white stucco work, it's a picture of the Countess Markievicz by her husband Casimir. It's not like the solid paintings of public men and patriots elsewhere in Leinster House. This one is private, wistful somehow, as though both sitter and artist knew that life would bring loss and separation.

It did. Casimir and Constance grew apart. She, despite being the first woman to be elected to either the British or Irish parliament, and to be a cabinet minister, has been quietly lost in the mists of time, and now Lissadell, her family's home in Ireland, has been sold.

Now, she was a notice-box and a trouble-maker. She was a one-woman riot. Maybe women have learned that that is the way to get things done. Indeed, according to Jacqueline Van Voris in *Constance de Markievicz: In the Cause of Ireland*, she burned the Union Jack on the day of King George's coronation and caused a riot. On the same day, when the police tried to arrest nationalist speakers in Foster Place, she leaped onto the wagonette to which the platform was attached, grabbed the reins and galloped the horses, platform speakers and all up to Stephen's Green. Early in her career, she would arrive sometimes to meetings of Inghinidhe na hÉireann (Daughters of Érin, the organisation founded by Maud Gonne to promote Irish independence, economy and culture) in full evening dress from some reception in the castle. She loved dressing up, both as an actress in her husband's plays and in her Fianna and Citizen Army uniform.

And it is often this histrionic and lady-of-the-manor side of her that is remembered, rather than the woman who fed starving strikers during the 1913 lock out, who fought in Stephen's Green during the 1916 rising and who spent long spells in jail.

But she was a socialist; she did care about the poor, both as the first Minister for Labour and as a woman who hauled sacks of turf she'd begged from friends up to shivering old people in the Dublin slums. Over the years prison and politics took their toll on her beauty. Her friend Mary Colum, quoted by Van Voris, said: 'She was haggard and old, dressed in ancient, demoded clothes … The familiar eyes that blinked at me from behind glasses were bereft of the old fire and eagerness.'

She was treated with scorn by the new Free State, not very keen on all the things she was: feminist, socialist and republican. It is said that on hunger strike outside a prison where Republican prisoners were being held, she yelled at the governor on the way out (he was Philip Cosgrave, brother of WT): 'British hireling, Irish traitor, let them go. Arrest me!' He is said to have replied: 'Madam, British hireling I may be. Irish traitor I may be. But I am not a collector of curiosities.'

When she died in 1927, at almost sixty years old, the new Free State was mean about her funeral. They wouldn't let her lie in state in the Mansion House or City Hall, but the poor of Dublin lined the streets to see her hearse pass by.

At the end of her life, she was isolated. Her beloved sister Eva, also a socialist and feminist in England, died the year before. At that stage she hadn't seen her brother since 1917 and said understandingly of him: 'I suppose it's very embarrassing to have a relation that gets into jail and fights in revolutions you are not in sympathy with.'

The family at Lissadell had paid a price for her activities. As her niece Gabriela explained to RTÉ's 'Seven Days' in 1970, the family had been ostracised by their own Anglo-Irish class after 1916, and had led lonely lives as a result. She said they were Irish in England and English in Ireland, and they had Madame's constant problem: 'Often, the accent of our voice annoys people,' she said sadly. 'But that's how we are. We can't do anything about that.'

The family weren't republican but neither were they unionist. They had helped finance Parnell; they were Home Rulers. In any case, as Irish citizens, they deserved better than the treatment they got from the Irish state. The state was put in charge of Lissadell in the forties when the then heir, Sir Michael Gore-Booth, was declared a ward of court due to mental illness. The Gore-Booths claimed that during that time timber was sold from which the estate did not benefit. That wonderful 'Seven Days' investigation, presented by Denis Mitchell and produced by Colm Ó Briain, should be shown again now, just to remind us of how careless we are with our history and with those we pretend to revere.

Maybe it will remind us, too, why we should try to keep some public access to Lissadell, to embrace it and all who belonged to it no matter what their political views, no matter what their accents. Not just for its charming shabbiness; for Casimir's murals of waiters carrying laden trays in the dining room; or for the drawing room with, as Yeats describes them, 'the great windows open to the south'. Not just for the letter from the local parish priest thanking the family for going into debt to feed their tenants during the famine. For all these things, but also, for 'two girls in silk kimonos, both beautiful, one a gazelle'.

A Better Class of Person

'You know, Mick knows nothing about Shakespeare,' sniffed a Ukrainian stable girl recently about her Irish stable-boy colleague. They both work for one of Ireland's leading horse trainers, but the difference with the Ukrainians is their education. Like the Irish, they love horses. They come from the great Cossack tradition, and some of them would have been part of the old Soviet-subsidised Cossack groups who gave displays of daredevil riding at state fairs around the USSR. There's no subsidy now and they've had to come here to work and to learn to ride short – jockey style, like Irish race-riders. But there's one way they still score over their Irish co-workers – most have third-level qualifications.

That's true of many of the 200,000 foreign immigrants who have come to Ireland since the mid-nineties, making up about 5% of the population. A small number of those are asylum-seekers. A much bigger percentage comes in on work visas – which apply mostly to nursing and medical staff – and work permits. And where are they coming from? Well, looking at the work permits issued this year alone, they come from all over but above all from the Philippines, Latvia, Lithuania, Poland, and the Ukraine. Where are they working? In agriculture, horticulture and related industries like meat processing; in catering; in construction; in health and other services.

And what do they bring? Well, the first thing many of them bring is education. A recent survey by the 'Interact' group showed that more immigrant than Irish workers had third-level degrees. You'd expect this in the health services, but it also applied in the food-processing and catering industries. This is education – human capital – to invest in our economy, even though much of the time we haven't allowed them to use it. We've used them instead as waitresses, stable boys, mushroom pickers, and without them our tourist and horse-racing and horticultural industries would have hit serious difficulties in the last three years. With the wages they get at home, they're happy to work at more menial jobs here even if it means, as in one company in County Meath, solicitors and journalists working as waste sorters.

So far, we haven't allowed them to flex their muscles, except in areas like the health services where we desperately need them. We've tried to keep them in boxes. We've let employers control their work permits which, as Mary Robinson said at an Immigrant Council of Ireland conference, condemns them to a form of bondage, of slavery. Some of them have decent employers who help them learn English, who look out for them.

But others live in barely converted sheds and outhouses, terrified to make contact with unions and sacked if they do. Many are isolated and afraid of their own mafia and unaware of their rights. One young woman was told by a fellow Latvian that she would have to pay him to get her a PPS number. The union told her all she had to do was ring up the factory she used to work for and they would give her the PPS number. When they did, she was delighted and turned to the union man and said, 'Now, what do I pay you?' People like that are easily preyed upon, easily abused, and a long-term, more constructive immigration policy would help.

But from May 2004, in many ways, that will change. The ten new countries, with up to seventy-five million people, who join the EU will be given immediate access to Ireland from day one. That means that people from countries like Latvia, Lithuania, Poland and other East European countries will be able to come here with their families and compete for the sort of jobs they are well qualified to do, just as English or French people can. They will become a permanent part of our society, not guest workers as we've forced them to be up to now. And that should be our attitude to immigrants, even to those who are not part of the EU – that they will be part of us, not just passers-through.

In Canada, they have a sign at the airport which says to immigrants, 'Welcome to your country'. And it is that attitude, the expansionist attitude of North America, rather than the colonialist attitude of old Europe, which we should be adopting. As former US Congressman Bruce Morrison puts it, we shouldn't see immigration as some sort of charity. Immigrants are the triers, the achievers, the entrepreneurs who energise a society and an economy.

Look at this country now compared to the monochrome 1950s. Look at the colour, the flavours, the Indian and Chinese restaurants, the African food stores, and spotted up near the Sinn Féin Offices in Parnell Square: the sign in English and Cyrillic for the Russian Food Company Cash and Carry.

They've changed us, and their energy and their skills are going to fuel the growth in this country in future years. And we've had our effect on them, too. The other day a man approached me wearing a Muslim skullcap. He looked as though he could have been from Iraq, or from Egypt, but when he opened his mouth, his broad Dublin accent told me exactly where he was from.

And he's the future. It will be different. It will be exciting. And, it will still be Ireland.

Through Irish Eyes

It was ten years ago and she worked with me in Yorkshire Television. She was a first-class journalist, who had researched and scripted award-winning programmes, and now she wanted me to narrate her script for another one.

'Why don't you do it yourself?' I asked. 'It's your work and you have a lovely voice.'

'No,' she said in her cut-glass Home Counties tones. 'They don't want people with my accent any more.'

And that's when I knew how much relations had changed between Britain and Ireland, when my Irish accent was more acceptable for a British audience than that of a well-bred English girl. Now, there was an element of political correctness in operation here. Irish accents are regarded as classless in Britain and therefore useful. Still, it was a change from ten years earlier, when I was working for the BBC's 'Newsnight', and we would get complaints from the public if Scotsman Donald MacCormick and myself presented the programme together. One bloody Celt was bad enough, we were told, but two!

I mention the whole business of Irish-British relations because of a report which records an historic new warmth in Irish attitudes towards the British. 'Through Irish Eyes', a survey carried out in Ireland for the British Embassy and the British Council, shows that four out of five Irish people regard relations with Britain as very good and improved, particularly over the last decade.

It's been a difficult relationship, complicated by the colonial hangover, by Northern Ireland, by the IRA bombing campaign. But now Britain's colonial times are all but over, as is the IRA campaign of violence. Our increased prosperity means that the daily lives of Irish and British people are quite similar now and we watch many of the same TV programmes and football teams. The old suspicions and hatreds are fading and we're all better off for that.

But differences still remain. One thing which still irritates me, for instance, is the extent to which we are invisible to the British. On BBC Radio 4's 'Start the Week' one morning there was a discussion about immigration into Britain since the last war. Of all the nationalities mentioned, there was no mention of Ireland, despite the massive influx of Irish people, particularly in the fifties, and the fact that the Irish are the biggest ethnic group in England after the English. Why are we invisible? Well, it may be partly because we can travel without passports to Britain and so are different to other foreigners; or it may be because the British have forgotten we ever left them.

The survey shows that in some ways we still find the British arrogant, and it is true that they assume their way is always best and things foreign are suspect. I mean, have you noticed the horror with which a London taxi driver reacts to a stray euro cent in your change as though it was going to give him avian flu or something?

And then there's that accent – and yes, I know, I'm making the assumption that all British people come from the Home Counties, which isn't fair. But when actor Stephen Rea was advised by Sir Peter Hall to advance his career by switching his Belfast tones for a proper English accent, he refused. He said it would limit him too much because it was an accent which squeezed out all emotion. It was the necessary tool of a ruling class. And yes, that accent is less dominant, less the voice of official Britain than it used to be, but the hankering after more glorious times is still there. And that nostalgia for empire which is ruefully recognised by the British themselves was sent up something rotten by Ricky Gervais of the TV series 'The Office' addressing a US audience at the Golden Globe

Awards. 'I'm from a little place called England,' he said wistfully. 'We used to run the world before you.'

But if *their* empire annoys us, *our* empire annoys them. One English friend, an atheist, who's been living here for decades pointed it out: 'There's a pervasive Catholic cultural supremacy here, even still, and even lapsed Catholics aren't really aware of it. The radio discussion about the Church's handling of complaints of clerical abuse will run right up to six o'clock and then the presenter will say: "Now, we pause for the Angelus." I mean, come on. Don't you even notice it?' He was astonished at the way his children were automatically prepared for First Communion at national school, and his son recruited as an altar boy, without anyone talking to him first. He didn't like the way the local priest just walked into his house.

Fair enough, and that wouldn't happen in Britain. I like the British and I love working with them. They're organised, conscientious, appreciative, truthful. They are often more interested in ideas than people; they don't let emotions and personalities get in the way – they concentrate on making the final product as good as it can be. Great people to work with. But what about living with them?

Well, I also remember being asked to dinner in London by broadcasting friends. After dinner we retired to the sitting room and the conversation sagged. So we, the two Irish people, sat over to the piano and sang a few songs. No one joined in. In desperation, we tried a few old faithfuls, even resorting to 'Molly Malone' and 'Danny Boy'. The English sat and listened politely. So we gave up and went home.

Next day, we bumped in to all the dinner-party people. 'That was wonderful last night,' they said. 'Live music. So spontaneous. We haven't had such fun for ages.'

We gaped at them and turned away pityingly. You know, sometimes you have to feel sorry for the poor old Brits.

ATONEMENT

Good Night, Sisters

I had an English teacher called Gussie, Sister Augustine, as round and bouncy as a rubber ball. Gussie was a child of the jazz age and she believed in everything American. She taught Shakespeare as though he was Damon Runyon and his plays were peopled by guys and dolls. We loved her. We were rarely late for Gussie's class but if we were, she'd tip her veil like George Raft would tip the brim of his hat, point you to your seat and drawl, 'Get parked, babe.'

Gussie was only one of a set of brilliant teachers: Matthew, who recited poetry like a woman in love; Assumpta, who opened us up to the *Aeneid*; Michael, who showed us that music can help make life worth living. Yes, I was one of those who benefited from a religious institution. Girls like me from modest backgrounds were educated for a pittance by dedicated women who focused all their energy and their ambition on us.

In recent times, though, I've had to remember that while we flourished in our school, other children in residential homes, run by religious, led stunted lives, lives of ritual humiliation and even of horrific abuse. The system which helped me, damaged them, sometimes irreparably, and the reckoning had to come.

Going back to my time at school, I remember that one of the things I didn't like was being told about the superior nature of the religious vocation. Some were called to marriage, we were told, but that was a lesser vocation. The arrogance of this stunned me – the presumption that those of us outside religious orders were less moral, less spiritual, that we would always need them to lead the way. That arrogance continues in the brokering of an indemnity deal with the state over abuse in religious-run institutions, which saves their skin at a potentially great cost to the rest of us.

Why did the state go along with it? Why couldn't the state on its own pay compensation to those abused by its agents, the religious? Why couldn't the state then sue the orders as I gather has been done elsewhere. Wouldn't that be a clearer approach? But the orders would go bankrupt, you say. Yes, maybe they would, and that would mean they would have to sell off property.

They might also be forced to divest themselves of their holdings in, taking Dublin alone, the Mater, Saint Vincent's, Temple Street Hospital, the Rehabilitation Institute, which if the state had to buy them could cost hundreds of millions alone, depending on the terms of the trusteeships. The religious would have to pull out of the many long-term care institutions for the old and the mentally handicapped which they help to run. Those who could would have to support themselves in the workplace and the bulk of the 11,000 members of the religious orders in the country who are over sixty would fall to the state to provide for.

So it would cost us. But it will also cost us to have the state taking the brunt of cases against which the religious are now indemnified. Much of the taking over of institutions run by religious orders and replacement of their labour is going to be happening anyway as vocations disappear – so wouldn't this merely accelerate the process? Anyway, is it the job of the state to prop up religious orders and protect them from the arm of justice? Maybe they *should* go bankrupt. Maybe the heavens *should* fall. And maybe that's best, for the Roman Catholic Church, for all of us.

Stepping in to preserve the religious orders from their own sins presumes that the rest of us aren't capable of running a decent society, that we will always need the religious to help us. It continues to treat us as children, as the Church always has. Maybe it's time that we, that our state, took our full responsibility.

Where would that leave the Church? Well, I remember asking the respected theologian, Enda McDonagh, how he felt about a collapse of the present system of hierarchical institutional Church. He must always welcome change, he said simply, partly because he's a scientist, fired by the possibility of discovery, by the trust that change will bring something new, something better.

That's what may come from a destruction of the present system – a more adult society, and a smaller but more adult, more accountable Church, both of which will be a better place for all our friends who are religious. I think of mine, particularly of the nuns, friends from school, friends from my home town: Anne, and Sheila, and Joanna, and Brigid and Helena, all people who would add to any society. To quote the Blessed Nell McCafferty, maybe it's 'Good night, sisters.' Maybe it's the end, but maybe it's also the beginning.

Digging up Old Monks

The English are a very literal people – they think you mean exactly what you say. Talking to two English friends once about my grandfather, I told them he was a baker but that in his spare time he dug up old monks. They stared at me horrified. 'You mean,' said one sympathetically, 'that he was a bit strange, a sort of necrophiliac?' Well, no I didn't. I meant that in his spare time he was an amateur archaeologist and pottered around old abbeys.

But once he actually did dig up old monks. He was building new bakery ovens at his home in Graignamanagh, and in the walls they discovered a sort of catacomb with the skeletons of monks. The house, you see, was built onto the back of the thirteenth-century Cistercian Abbey of Duiske. Half of Graignamanagh is like that – a beautiful old town whose houses cling like barnacles to the rock of a medieval abbey. It's a bit like the society we've grown up in, with a past so inextricably attached to the Catholic Church that you stumble over it no matter what direction you strike out in. So it's part of us and what made us, no matter how much we might now like to deny it.

Yes, we're back to that abuse deal again, because if the Church and the religious orders deal bravely with the specific allegations of abuse now facing them, it could help all of us come to terms with the wounds left by what was an extraordinarily abusive society. It's not just the compensation money that matters. It's the truth. Those who deal with people who have suffered abuse say that what they want above all else is to have their story heard – to have their story heard and to get an acknowledgement by the abusers, or those who represent them, of what has happened. That acknowledgement of responsibility allows the abused finally to take back power over their own lives.

There is no South African-type Truth and Reconciliation Commission to which they can tell their story. They only have the Commission to Inquire into Child Abuse, which is why the government's attempt to take only sample cases to the Commission was repressive because it stifled individual stories. It remains to be seen whether Mr Justice Ryan's proposals to have cases heard in groups will also stifle those important individual voices.

But the religious too must accept that the telling of the truth is the most important thing. They must confront the anger that's out there, not hide from it. You could hear that anger on all the phone-in radio programmes about children in institutions, and about the treatment of women in the Magdalen laundries. Caller after caller compared the miserable lives of the Magdalens with the fine nursing homes and private health care provided for the ageing nuns.

And that's what so many of those who've come through institutions see: the religious providing for themselves, but hiding behind lawyers when it comes to facing up to providing for those against whom they, or members of their orders, have sinned in the past. They took the legal instead of the pastoral route. It has created difficulties between the eighteen orders involved in the abuse, and the over 100 or so other orders in the Conference of Religious of Ireland. The eighteen, it is believed, expect solidarity from the others while not being ready to talk about the situation. But it's affecting the work of all the other orders, including the work of CORI's Justice Commission whose secretary, Father Seán Healy, has suggested the eighteen orders involved should open up their books. Indeed, new legislation for registered charities will require that that be done.

The deal-makers, Sister Elizabeth Maxwell and Sister Helena O'Donoghue, have been profiled in the papers as redoubtable women, Iron Ladies of the Cloth, invulnerable. The problem with invulnerable people, however, is that often they don't listen.

They might learn from a man in Ennis who has often been called a fool. He's the Bishop of Killaloe, Willie Walshe. He invites evicted traveller families to park on his lawn, and down the line there are problems, and people say, 'I told you so.' He does a penitential walk to atone for the Church's sins, and people say he'd be better off in his office catching up on paperwork. But he does something very important. Firstly, he listens. Secondly, he does and says what he thinks is right even if he's laughed at, even if it makes him vulnerable, as vulnerable as all the people round him. And maybe that makes him a fool. And maybe there's such a thing as being God's Fool.

IRAQ

Tony's War

My dad brought us to a hurling match when I was small. Borris wasn't doing very well and eventually there was a bad-tempered scrap. The opposition emerged limping, and as a result one of our guys was sent off. 'Good man, Jimmy!' roared a Borris man in front of us. 'You hit something anyway.'

I suppose that's what the US did with Iraq. You can't score against Osama Bin Laden so why not take the opportunity to beat up a few old enemies instead. The quantum leap from Bin Laden and September 11 to Iraq was breathtaking, but the western world was dragged along with it. Some were dragged, but some jumped way ahead. I was fascinated by the sight of Tony Blair, a British Labour Prime Minister, out there barking for a war. He made it clear he was always ready to go ahead, even without a second UN mandate. His Home Secretary Jack Straw, former head of the British students' union and once up to his neck in anti-Vietnam war protests, went around warning that 'patience' with Saddam was running out. Bloodthirsty or what?

I suppose what we forget is that Britain is a military nation, no matter who its prime minister is. I remember when working there being struck by the importance given to things military. In the office at BBC's 'Newsnight', people became as excited as children at the prospect of a military story: 'Let's drag in a few brass hats tonight, what?' burbled one happy presenter. There was a reverence shown to the security forces that we in Ireland once showed to the Church, a sense that the military defined Britain in a way that the Catholic Church once defined us. A government only had to murmur the words 'national security' and the whole establishment backed whatever D-notice or emergency measure the military required.

This happened with Labour as much as the Conservatives. Harold Wilson backed Lyndon Johnson on Vietnam. Left-winger Michael Foot raised hardly a murmur about the Falklands War.

If anything, Labour Secretaries of State in Northern Ireland were more identified with the security forces than were their conservative counterparts – remember Roy Mason?

With Tony Blair, you wonder whether it's partly a rite of passage. It seems like every British prime minister has to have his war, has to have those pictures of him in shirtsleeves meeting British troops in faraway places, those distant echoes of 'In which we serve', those even more distant echoes of empire. Margaret Thatcher had hers in the Falklands; John Major had his in the Gulf War. Now Tony's had his turn.

But Tony doesn't usually take risks with the voters. He's careful. As a promising Labour frontbencher in 1992 I remember he would always refuse to do the long interview on programmes like BBC's 'On the Record'. Four-and-a-half minutes was his limit, he confided to a producer friend. After that, he knew he'd be forced to say something which might alienate somebody.

So why did this poll-driven prime minister take this hawkish stance, sending a quarter of the British army to the Middle East when the polls showed that 50% of the public were against a war and 80% were against a war without a second UN resolution? Why did he sound as though he was talking to a US electorate rather than to a British one?

Perhaps it's because that may be the truth of it – that he feels he doesn't have to worry about the vote at home. So he's turning his mind to developing a profile as an international statesman. He could have played that role in the EU if British public opinion on the euro had allowed him to. But he knows that it may take some time, if ever, to pass a referendum, and France and Germany will ensure he's marginalised as long as the UK is outside the euro.

Only the US stage allows him to do a bit of international swash-buckling, to talk about 'rattling Saddam', to get into war huddles with President Bush. It would seem that Tony Blair may be devoting the last part of his prime ministerial career to vanity politics. One had hoped for more.

Peace Tourists

It was the 'Bush and Blair Show', just like one of those creepy husband-and-wife programmes, where the presenter who's not speaking looks adoringly at the one who is. Bush, like a really bad actor, stared unblinkingly at Tony Blair. Behind them as much red, white and blue as you'll meet on the Twelfth of July. Around them as many administration celebrities as you'd meet in a war edition of *Hello* magazine.

It was Tony's party at Hillsborough but Tony knew his place. He referred deferentially to his American colleague as 'President Bush'. The president, cosily, called him 'Tony', America's firmest friend. Bush looked like a man who rarely loses sleep. The British Prime Minister, pale under his make-up, showed the strain of being America's firmest friend.

There was, for instance, the whole business of ensuring that the US allowed the UN a role in post-war Iraq. Not easy. As one American pundit put it on 'Morning Ireland', describing the hawkish attitude in the Pentagon, 'We don't want messy other people getting in the way.' Messy other people presumably means the UN, and the role the President saw for the UN was clearly one of handing out food and medicine and, he said, having some contribution to the Interim Iraqi Administration, whatever that means. But the President said he wanted his sceptics in Europe to be in no doubt that when he said there would be a vital role for the UN, he meant it. 'I mean what I say,' he said. 'Saddam knows I mean what I say!'

It was an unfortunate lapse into triumphalism, one Tony Blair was careful not to follow. After all, this was the summit which both the US and the UK calculated would turn George W Bush from a war president into a peace president. Yup – just like that. You draw a line from Afghanistan through Iraq, through a Middle East peace plan, to the peace process in Northern Ireland and there you have it: Mr Bush the Peacemaker.

OK, there were some warlike outbursts from George W, like the one about how he was removing the hand of Saddam from the throat of the Iraqi people: 'I can't tell you if all ten fingers are off the throat, but the fingers are coming off one by one.' But then he was nudged back to script about how all the communities in Northern Ireland should seize the plan for peace, and how participation in the process would have reverberations well beyond Northern Ireland, ie, in the Middle East and Iraq.

Northern Ireland is where American presidents come to be hailed as peacemakers. Bill Clinton showed that, and this little trip was the least Tony Blair could do for his firmest ally, President Bush. Was the Irish government consulted at all before Bush came? That's not clear. Did the President visit the Republic as Clinton always did? Nope. But the Irish government wasn't complaining about this use of the North as a handy peace backdrop for Bush. Arriving at Hillsborough, Bertie Ahern leaned in purposefully and grasped George W's arm like an old buddy and the President arm-grasped him back. Bertie is a man who easily links Irish and Middle Eastern issues. Wasn't it Bertie, after all, who referred to Temple Bar, with its Bohemian lifestyle, as Dublin's West Bank?

There were lots of pretty TV pictures in the sunshine, with rhododendrons at Hillsborough giving lovely spring colour. And lots of colourful pictures from Iraq, like last night's BBC ten o'clock news with British troops cheerfully breaking down the carved double doors of Saddam's palace in Basra. 'It wasn't exactly palace etiquette,' burbled the reporter in the upbeat tones of a Second

World War newsreel. Then came shots of gold taps, gilded chairs, patterned marble floors – and soldiers eagerly examining them. All great fun.

What we didn't see too much of was the real currency of war: the dead bodies; the hospitals overrun with wounded children; and men and women barely alive with bloody holes blown through them. Neither did talk of death and injury figure much in the 'Bush and Blair Show' – a bit too messy, perhaps, just like the Pentagon's determination not to be bothered by messy other people.

And after it all, Mr Bush was pleased. As the two men walked off set after their press conference, the President turned to the British Minister and beamed, touching his arm. 'Good jawb,' murmured George W Bush to his good friend, Tony. 'Good jawb.'

The End of History

It was a piece of history all right. They were all there: de Valera, JFK, Benjamin Franklin and even Francis Fukiyama, all brought in to support one side or the other, except that Dev was brought in by Fine Gael and Francis Fukiyama was brought in by … well, wait for it … Bertie Ahern.

Now maybe it might have been better if Francis was left at home, because no sooner had Bertie uttered the words 'the end of history' than Michael D Higgins' nose was quivering. You don't play the game of intellectual one upmanship with Michael D without expecting trouble. So, as though over the dumbest boy in the sociology class, Michael D poured fine scorn over the outbreak of severe existentialism in Fianna Fáil. But in fact, he pointed out, the Taoiseach, in quoting Francis Fukiyama might have unwittingly found the true source of present American foreign policy. The arguments for an attack on Iraq had been carried as far back as 1997 on a website 'Project for a New American Century', to which both Defence Secretary Donald Rumsfeld and Francis Fukiyama, he said, contributed.

The press were waiting all day for Michael D. He's one of the few speakers, like the late John Kelly, or Des O'Malley, who can fill the press gallery and even some of the Dáil benches. When he rose to speak it was vintage stuff, a sharp grasp of the detail with a fine mix of scorn and anger and all, of course, without a note. 'Why do you bother with notes at all?' a colleague asked him. 'Why,' replied Michael D airily, 'to wave them about, to wave them about, you know.'

It was a fascinating day with a real sense that deputies enjoyed tackling a bigger topic. The diplomatic box was full and even parliamentary ghosts of past battles, Michael Noonan, and Beverly Cooper-Flynn, appeared among the benches.

The Taoiseach was in a difficult position. In government, he's decided to be pragmatic about Shannon, but it is hard to make an eloquent speech when you are regretting war on one hand and defending, on the other, the facilitating at Shannon of one of the belligerents.

But really it was Enda's day. Fine Gael hasn't been consistent about much in recent years, but on the question of war against Iraq, Kenny has been adamant: no use of Shannon without a second UN resolution for war.

He used every available Leaders' Question Time to push the government on their attitude to the war and make clear his own. Fine Gael, the law and order party, thinks law and order in the world is best defended by the UN and this war undermines the UN. It was a quiet and simple performance but it carried with it the weight of a view consistently held.

Dick Roche and Noel Treacy set themselves up as the government hecklers – Tweedledum and Tweedledee, both red-faced, white-haired and bespectacled, and both equally ineffective. They should take lessons from Brian Cowen. Cowen sat there all day, giving opposition speakers the evil eye: sometimes openly contemptuous, his jaw dropping in disbelief. When Caoimhghín Ó Caoláin of Sinn Féin stood up, he'd had enough. When Ó Caoláin begged that weapons of mass destruction should be decommissioned, Cowen barked: 'It never happened in your party.'

Mary Harney and Conor Lenihan defended America passionately, as our friends to whom we would not deny comfort now. Trevor Sargent of the Greens and Socialist Joe Higgins spoke of the Iraqi blood to be spilled.

But you know, mused one journalist colleague, it wouldn't make a blind bit of difference what was said or done, the government position wouldn't change. They would still facilitate the US at Shannon, whether the UN did or didn't give a mandate for war. One government speaker spoke of the wrong war at the wrong time. Ah, so that was the government position, we concluded, a bit like the song: 'It's the wrong war, at the wrong time, but baby, it's all right with me.'

DARKNESS AND LIGHT

What You Don't Know Can Hurt You

A colleague in *The Irish Times* was driving into work past Dublin Airport some years ago when he saw a plane career off the runway. He got to a nearby phone box and rang the airport information officer. 'Can you tell me,' he asked, 'about the Jumbo which came off the runway today?' No Jumbo, he was told, had come off the runway. 'Ah, come on,' said my colleague, 'sure I'm looking at it with my own eyes.' 'Ah!' said the information officer. 'You mean *that* Jumbo!'

The reluctance of public officials to give information is such that the introduction of the Freedom of Information Act must have seemed like being made to walk naked down Merrion Street. When it came in, in 1997, some threatened to stop writing things down so that when the file was released in response to a request under the FOI, there would be little in it. Politicians aren't much better about revealing information once they get into power. Indeed, the longer a government is in power, the more it has to hide and so it's no surprise that this coalition, in its second term, decided to close down on access to information by amending the act.

Now, why should anyone care about that? Charlie McCreevy put it with his usual grace when he said, 'This is only contentious for the media.' It's true that the public never gets as upset as does the press about issues of censorship. Journalists complained for years, for instance, about Section 31 of the Broadcasting Act which banned interviews with, among other groups, Sinn Féin, and no one cared tuppence. But the changes to the Freedom of Information Act, in an immediate and recognisable way, affect the public's daily right to know about matters relating to their own lives and affect what they learn through the media – and most of the information people glean is still through the media.

Basically, the act allowed the public and the press access to information about the way government and the state bodies did their business and came to decisions. It challenged the culture of secrecy in the public service and was even quoted by civil service reform bodies as evidence of how they had reformed.

Now it has been rolled back. Not only has the five-year delay on release of cabinet papers been extended to ten, but the definition of what constitutes a cabinet paper has been drastically widened, from papers created solely for government, to papers proposed to go before government. In other words, a document which might never reach cabinet at all could thereby be kept secret, or a document the authorities wanted to keep secret could, as happened in Australia, be simply passed across the cabinet table in order to give it cover. Correspondence between ministers and between civil servants can be withheld. It will be much more difficult to get information to do with EU negotiations, or negotiations with other governments. Also, the departmental advice behind answers to questions in the Dáil can now be withheld.

A whole series of overlapping reasons for withholding information are now being created and perhaps, most draconian of all, the right to appeal against a refusal to see policy papers can be refused where the process is certified as ongoing (and in government anything can be described as being ongoing). Since the act has been amended, introducing a charge for FOI requests which can go as high as €240 on appeal, the number of requests has fallen by over 80% in some departments.

So what sort of things do you now know about that you mightn't be allowed to know under the new act? Well, there's the proposed cost of the Bertie Bowl, for instance. The publicity helped to stop that expensive project in its tracks, an expense you, the taxpayer, would have borne. What else? Civil service concern at the cost of Special Savings and Investments Accounts was revealed and the publicity helped to cap what was going to be an economically expensive scheme. The rows between the ministers for Health and for Finance about the cost of the health services were revealed. The overcharging of people under the government's drugs refund scheme was revealed by an enterprising residents' group and people were compensated.

But what does all this stuff matter, you might ask, when set against more immediate matters like life and death, and war? Well, people need to be able to keep an eye on their governments, on their decisions in time of war, perhaps, more than at any other time.

Take the major controversy here over the landing and overflights of US military aircraft during the invasion of Iraq, mostly revealed by parliamentary questions and their background briefing information. Could that background information now be withheld, under more stringent regulations, because it involves negotiations and relations with other countries? That might very well suit the government, but wouldn't the rest of us like to know, feel we needed to know? Wouldn't you?

Let in the Light

Picture this. A man blunders into a consultant's room in a hospital. He gets thrown out. He wanders into an operating theatre. He turns up in the women's wards. He's a nuisance.

What's wrong with him? Well, he can't read. He can't read the notices. He can't read the signs. So he's afraid of going near a hospital again now in case he'll get lost.

A woman with a heart condition is given a diet and exercise regime to follow. It's all written out. She puts it in her pocket and does nothing about it because she can't read and she's too ashamed to ask for help.

These are just some of the stories which emerge from a recent study on literacy and the health services by the National Adult Literacy Agency. The problem, they point out, is that very often people with the poorest health, and the poorest health habits, are the people with the poorest literacy.

The ingenuity with which people get around their literacy problems indicates that the initial problem was not one of intelligence. But time and again they're caught out, like the woman who needed to buy thrift-pack foods in the supermarket but had to buy the dearer brands because they had pictures on the labels. Or the man who always bought a medicine off the shelf but was lost when the packet colour was changed.

The International Adult Literacy OECD study of some years ago showed that a quarter of Irish people of working age scored at the lowest literacy levels. The National Adult Literacy Agency and the VECs have been trying to address this problem at an adult level, but it's still coming through from the schools. Irish youngsters did well in a recent OECD study of fifteen-year-olds. But, you see, most of the kids with problems have left the school system by the time they are fifteen. We still have 6 to 8% of children coming to the end of primary schooling with serious literacy difficulties. They're mostly the ones who opt out of second level early and are most likely to be unemployed. They're the ones we're failing.

No child capable of reading or writing should leave primary school unable to do so. It shouldn't be allowed to happen. It should be our first educational priority. But without any form of assessment at primary level, or indeed until Junior Cert, how can we identify the vulnerable ones?

Some people argue for the return of the old Primary Certificate but, in fact, you need to be checking standards much earlier in the child's school life. Joe O'Toole, former INTO secretary and now President of Congress, has suggested assessments starting as early as six, involving first the teacher, and then a psychologist, and the parents. The important thing first is to identify the problem. There's been a reluctance to identify children who have difficulties for fear of stigmatising the child, or the school, or the teachers attached to the school. But only when you identify the vulnerable children will you be able to demand funds to help them. You'll need smaller classes so teachers have more time; you'll need more school psychologists; you may need more remedial teachers. So, you'll need more money, particularly for schools in disadvantaged areas.

That's why we have to have an honest debate about the allocation of education funds. That's why we must continue to question free university fees, and ask why the Labour Party insisted on introducing them. Let those who can afford to pay fees do so, and let the taxpayer subsidise those who can't. We spend much more per head on third level than on primary education – much more.

And yet it is the primary sector to which we have a constitutional duty and which is vital if equality of opportunity in education is ever to mean anything.

And yes, the third-level students will be out marching at the mention of any change in free fees. And they can make a lot of noise. And their mostly middle-class parents can make a lot of noise. But, if hard choices have to be made, think of the voices you don't hear, like the man who told literacy surveys that he had to keep turning down promotion because he couldn't fill in the time sheets; like the girl who couldn't write to her boyfriend abroad to tell him she loved him. And saddest of all, perhaps, because she wanted so little, was the woman who said: 'I just wanted to be able to read the newspaper.'

More than Cows

I met a farmer one day outside Dungarvan and he was a bit shy. So we were making conversation about his farm and his cattle. 'You have a few horses, too,' I said, as I heard the clip of hooves down the lane.

His face lit up. 'Ah, you'd have to,' he said. 'There's no romance in cows.'

His words came back to me as I was thinking about the forthcoming budget – that notion that all of us in life need something more than cows, something beautiful, whether it's an interest in music, or horses, or gardens, or books.

And how could I allow myself such flights of fancy when I should be shaking in my boots about some of the harsh news that Mr McCreevy might deliver? Well, I suppose it's partly because I'm older, old enough to remember the seventies, the 'squeeze 'em till the pips squeak' seventies when the marginal income tax rate soared over 70% and that was before the 10% surcharge – and think how quickly in this country you hit the marginal tax rate! And then there was the annual wealth tax, 1% on assets every year. It got to the stage where one senior Fine Gael minister, wanting to show off how rich he was, boasted that he was the sort of man who paid wealth tax. And there you have the story of the seventies. You couldn't have conspicuous consumption. So instead you had to impress the neighbours with conspicuous taxation – not that that level of taxation always achieves its target, of course. When taxation's that conspicuous, those who can will run and hide. And they did.

So if I had the Minister's ear, where would I start? Well, you'd start with what you'd have to do: raise the levels of support for those who have no other choice than to be dependent on the state. Personally, I'd give some hope to families of the mentally handicapped by increasing, not cutting, the number of residential places available. And when I was looking aghast at the 14% increase in the numbers of public servants in the last two years and at the cost of continuing to pay them, I'd remember that in there are those who care for the mentally handicapped, and do it with real care and commitment.

And the hard question: where would I tell him to cut? Well, I'm going to cop out; I'm not being paid his handsome salary so I'd rather tell him where not to cut.

And this is where we go back to romance, to the realisation that there is more to life than, well, cows. I'm talking about the feeling you get when you walk into the contemporary Irish art exhibition at the National Gallery; the feeling you have when the Abbey gets it right, as so often it does; and most of all, the feeling you get when you read a piece of poetry and it expresses, as never before, an essential truth. I suppose poetry above all distils down to the essence. Working with such bare bones, there's very little room for equivocation, for dissembling; poets, above all, have to be truthful. And at all times, but particularly when we're ill, or grief-stricken, or in despair, it's that essence, that truth, we thirst for.

For the people who write the stuff, too, it is a real process of distillation. Weeks, months, years of their lives go into one little book of work. Even a very successful collection will sell in hundreds rather than thousands. Poets mostly work at something else to subsidise what they do.

And that's why Charlie McCreevy should continue to give them their tax exemption. Even if he were to change the existing scheme (because I know it's felt that big-earning musicians and writers are well able to pay tax), why not take up the suggestion of a tax credit which would ensure that those artists earning less than, say, €50,000 a year would pay no income tax? We're talking here about playwrights, novelists, painters as well, but I'll stick to this final plea for poets:

Seamus Heaney, who is more generous to the public with his time and his presence than any great poet should have to be, has signed many a book, and when he signed one for me he wrote on it: 'Because poems help us to live.' Need I say any more?

Mr Right

I know a youngster who needed an escort to her deb's ball. So she got hold of the annual of a big Dublin boys' school, leafed through the photographs as though through a Goff's sales catalogue, until she found the best-looking senior boy. Then, though she didn't know him or anything about him, she invited him as her date. The dress, the shoes, the hair were right for the photograph and he would have to be right, too. It had to be, as the song says, perfect.

And 'perfect' is one of those words that divide the generations. In our time, we knew it would never be perfect, or even half perfect. We knew we were lucky to find anything in trousers at all, other than our brothers, to take us to our first dance. We knew as teenagers that spotty skin and a bit of puppy fat was something you lived with and, as the nuns might see it, part of nature's way of keeping us pure. We knew that we shouldn't complain about mousy hair because in the long term we wouldn't go grey as fast as those glossy brunettes and fast blondes. We knew, because we were told, that the pretty ones were never the brainy ones because God made sure that those of us who would not be sought in marriage would have our wits to fall back on.

Not any more. It has to be perfect. They want it all, beauty and brains, and they want it now. No one puts up with teenage spots – they take antibiotics and even stronger drugs. Figure-conscious teenagers join gyms at €700 a year. And as for the hair. Take the Arts faculties at the Dublin universities. One friend described going into a crowded lecture theatre. 'Every head was high-lighted,' she said. 'Women and men. It was like a peroxide rash.' Imagine thirty years ago as a student having the money to get your hair coloured! But now, for many middle-class kids, highlights,

Louis Vuitton bags, Karen Millen outfits, Chanel compacts are everyday items, partly paid for by adoring parents, but also from earnings from part-time jobs which would once have helped pay for university fees, but which now often finance the Armani jackets. '*Cosmo* is the bible,' said my university friend, 'and even if you are actually interested in your course, it's not cool to show it. One girl I know reads her Maths book inside the covers of *Cosmo*.'

It's a world where nobody waits anymore, where nobody saves for anything, not for holidays, not for cars, not for clothes. Why? Because the money is there; because parents in the swelling ranks of the Irish middle class have it; because youngsters are given loans and credit cards by the banks; because the notion of deferred gratification is quite alien. After all, if life now is all about consumption, then not to consume is perhaps not to live. That puts pressure on middle-class kids because the consumption is ultimately unsatisfying, and terrible pressure on poorer kids because they can't even join in the game.

And where does this search for perfection through consumption come from? Well, it's the search which drives the engine of capitalism and it comes from the American notion that we have the right to be happy now, that heaven and perfection can be had on this earth. The British, being a pessimistic lot, have never put much store in happiness, but the Americans regard it as their birthright. And this generation of Irish youngsters regard it as their birthright too.

And being older, and of the 'Valley of Tears' generation, doesn't mean I don't remember what it was like to be an eighteen-year-old student and going to your first big dance and wanting it to be just right. I wasn't worried about the fella; I was worried about the dress. I was a scholarship girl at Loreto Hall on Stephen's Green and every day I watched the dresses arriving in from the big Dublin stores knowing mine would be made down at home by Mrs Murphy who made our school uniforms and who was great but a bit ... well old-fashioned. When she gave me my first fitting in her tidy parlour looking out on the farmyard, Mrs Murphy was very dubious about the Empire-line dress. 'Sure, the waist is right up under the child's bust, Mrs O'Leary,' she said to my mother. 'That can't be right.' 'Just follow the pattern, Mrs Murphy,' said my mother firmly.

On the day of the dance, I went down to collect it off the Graignamanagh bus and sneaked it in, bound in brown paper and masses of string, past all the elegant dress bags from Richard Alan's and Switzers. Gloomily, I pulled it on and padded in my stockinged feet down to the long mirror in the hall. And there it was, the most beautiful dress in the world, white and fluid and shimmering. And I can still remember how I felt and how I blessed Mrs Murphy of Ballymurphy. In the middle of teenage spots and insecurities and fears there was one shining night of my life that she had made, well, just ... perfect.

NORTH OF THE BORDER

New Territory

Sometimes it seems like nothing ever changes in Northern Ireland, that everything is caught in a time warp. I remember, long after Jack Lynch had stopped being Taoiseach, I was referred to by Paisleyites in the North as 'the girl from Jack Lynch's radio'. Quaint, you might say, sweet in its way, unless you were stuck on the bridge in Derry in the middle of a Unionist protest march with Paisleyite women shouting: 'She's from Jack Lynch's radio. Throw her into the river, into the river!' I fled for protection to the Reverend Martin Smith. I knew I was safe with Martin.

In the North nothing changes and yet everything has changed, and it has its effect down here. The latest rustling in the undergrowth, and that for the moment is all it may be, is the talk of parties in the Republic organising in Northern Ireland. At its 2002 conference, the Labour Party passed a motion asking its National Executive to develop Labour Party branches and structure in the North. Fianna Fáil passed a similar Ard-Fheis motion to organise and contest elections on a 32-county basis, and the Taoiseach said that Fianna Fáil had to be conscious of the fact that the dynamic and the context of politics on this island had changed.

So does this mean that the poor old SDLP in the North, which has long fought the good fight for peaceful politics, is going to be taking a battering in the future not only from Sinn Féin but also from its old friends in the Republic? Well, let's put it in context. Labour has changed its constitution to allow Labour support groups to be set up in the North. These won't contest elections. They are really being created to allow a sort of pavilion membership of the party for all those Northerners who had nowhere to go when they left the Workers' Party (formerly Official Sinn Féin) with the creation of the 26-county Democratic Left, which is now subsumed into the Labour Party. This satisfies a short-term need, but it doesn't mean that in the longer term the goal of organising and contesting elections in the North won't be pursued on the National Executive by Sligo's Declan Bree, who has always argued that socialists need a more leftwing option than what he sees as the overly nationalist SDLP.

After all, he argues, the trade union movement is organised on a 32-county basis and Labour used to have a 32-county organisation, with an MP at Stormont, Jack Beattie, who was also a Westminster MP, and councillors in the strongholds of Newry and Warrenpoint and even Derry. It was with the creation of the Social Democratic and Labour Party in 1970 that Labour instructed its branches in the North to become SDLP branches and retreated from the North.

Former leader, Ruairí Quinn, a staunch supporter of the SDLP, however, says it would be unfriendly to compete with the SDLP and it would damage them.

Fianna Fáil, having voted to organise in the North, has kicked the matter off to a committee of the National Executive where it may remain for some time. De Valera again and again resisted attempts by the old Nationalist Party in the North to team up with Fianna Fáil. There were rumours at one stage, because of the perceived close relationship between Charles Haughey and Seamus Mallon, that some sort of merger might be mounted but there's always been sharp resistance within the SDLP to any alignment with a party in the Republic. It prefers to have good relations with all of them, says they have been supportive, and says diplomatically that it has no doubt they will continue to be supportive.

In the end, however, political parties are about power. If Fianna Fáil and Labour perceive danger, they will look to their own interests first. And right now Sinn Féin has overtaken the SDLP in the North and is nibbling away at support for Fianna Fáil and Labour in the Republic. It may suit the Southern parties at least to threaten to compete with Sinn Féin in the Northern heartland. They will be looking to the long-term, and will be concerned about a 32-county Ireland where Sinn Féin are suddenly a massive political presence. They know the decline of the SDLP will leave too easy a vacuum for Sinn Féin to fill.

But for the moment Fianna Fáil, in particular, will worry about fragmenting the nationalist vote. After all, it's still the North and politics is still sectarian. There are some things which never change.

The Price of Peace

Watching Ian Paisley ramming his November 2003 election victory, as he would describe it, 'down the thick gullets' of the media, one was reminded how much he loves the public Punch and Judy show. He particularly enjoyed clashing with us, the Southern media. At first, he wouldn't come into studio for us; we had to follow him with a camera on the street while he shouted answers and insults at us across the heads of his supporters. It all made for dramatic television, so we didn't mind.

But it didn't always suit him to play Doctor No. I remember interviewing him in 1979 for the Canadian Broadcasting Corporation. I arrived late because my car had broken down, and I waited for the usual rant. It didn't come. There was tea and biscuits and a statesmanlike hour-long interview in which he spoke of good relations with Dublin and the need to include both communities. When I left, he wished me well and called after me: 'And would you ever get yourself a better car!'

'You're dead right, Dr Paisley,' I said, stepping into my poor old MG Midget. 'You can't trust these British cars.' Again, I waited for the rant, but it didn't come. He laughed and waved me off, and I drove away wondering what on earth had turned this roaring bull of a man into a jovial Santa Claus.

The answer, of course, was ambition. A window had suddenly opened for him and he could smell power. He had just topped the poll in the 1979 European elections, leaving the Official Unionists in third place. Suddenly a new British government, under Margaret Thatcher, was making overtures to him. Secretary of State Humphrey Atkins had a new plan which watered down power-sharing and excluded an Irish dimension, and Paisley was interested. People were talking of him as perhaps a future Prime Minister. He was already making conciliatory noises and preparing for the role.

Well, understandably, the SDLP wouldn't play ball. The window of opportunity closed, and Paisley may now say 'no' until the end of his career. Old men like to be consistent. But younger men are ambitious, as he once was. Peter Robinson and Nigel Dodds were seen to be first-class ministers and enjoyed being part of the executive. They'll want to do it again. They may well say 'no' for the next eighteen months, mopping up the Official Unionist vote in the European and local and general elections. But then, if Paisley, who'll be nearly eighty, goes, well, they may deal.

And who will they deal with? Well, Sinn Féin have been saying quietly for about three years that Trimble couldn't deliver, that they knew they'd have to deal with Donaldson and the DUP. It won't be easy for them and they won't like waiting eighteen months, but they too are on an electoral roll. They too have electoral mopping up to do and they're very, very good at that.

One observer passed their election caravan on the Falls Road a half-hour before the polls closed. They keep meticulous records, and voters, as they came out, reported to the caravan. Their names were ticked off, and absentees were spotted. Suddenly, an order was shouted to one of the cars standing outside at the ready, engines running. 'Go and get X. He's up in his mother's house hanging wallpaper. Bring him down here fast.'

Military men know how to run that sort of machine – that's how Fianna Fáil's developed. Sinn Féin will roll out that machine in elections north and south in 2004, in the Westminster elections in 2005, and perhaps in a general election here in 2006. One good friend in the North, an SDLP voter, was sad at Sinn Féin's triumph.

'Does this mean that half the people I know voted for them and maybe quietly always supported the terrible things they did?' she wondered. No, voters didn't always support the things they did. Women, in particular, didn't vote Sinn Féin as long as the IRA campaign continued. Sinn Féin got a reward from the voters for every move towards peace: after the 1994 ceasefire; after the 1998 Good Friday Agreement; after the decommissioning exercise before the Westminster elections of 2001; and again after the decommissioning in 2003. Their vote went up incrementally from 11% to 22% in that time. If they were to set off a bomb in the morning, they would lose it all. It's the price of peace.

And that may stick in the craw for some of us, but we're all in this together. Let's hope that there's a world out there for the younger ones, the ambitious ones, a world beyond the bitter old men, a world which is post-Provo and, oh yes please, post-Paisley.

Yannick
056-8958756
7.-45129542